OFF THE BOARDS

THE EVOLUTION OF ARCHITECTURAL PRACTICE

Dedication

This book is dedicated to Reagan, my love and encouraging muse; sons Richard and John, from whom I continue to learn; my colleagues at KBJ for their valuable support; and to future architects, that they may better see the road ahead by an occasional glance in the rear view mirror.

OFF THE BOARDS

THE EVOLUTION
OF ARCHITECTURAL PRACTICE

Richard T. Reep, Sr., AIA

FREEHAND PENCIL SKETCHES BY THE AUTHOR

Every effort has been made to trace all copyright-holders, but if any have been inadvertently overlooked, the publisher will be pleased to make the necessary arrangement at the first opportunity.

Copyright 2013 by Clemson University
ISBN 978-0-9835339-8-6

Published by Clemson University Press in Clemson, South Carolina

Editorial Assistant: Eva Stamm

To order copies, please visit the Clemson University Press website: www.clemson.edu/press.

Cover design by the author, adapted by Charis Chapman

Contents

List of Illustrations vi
Introduction viii

Chapter One: Boards 1
Chapter Two: Drawing 6
Chapter Three: Edges 18
Chapter Four: Scales 27
Chapter Five: CAD 33
Chapter Six: Documents 40
Chapter Seven: Images 48
Chapter Eight: Firms 56
Chapter Nine: Records 60
Chapter Ten: Design 67

A Note on the Author 80

List of Illustrations

K & E Thumbtacks 2
Drafting Dots 2
Work Station from the 1950s 3
Dazor Lamp 4
Drafting Stool 4
Spiroll Drawing Protector 5
Lego Blocks ca. 1970 6
Florida State College at Jacksonville, Downtown Campus, 1975.
    (RS&H Architects) 7
Wood Drafting Pencils 8
X-acto Knife with No. 11 Blade 8
Sanding Block 9
Leadholder 9
Package of B Leads 10
Pot Style Lead Pointer 10
Pentel Twist Erase with 0.5 mm Lead 11
Magic Rub eraser 12
Pink Pearl eraser 12
Electric Eraser 12
Erasing Shield 13
Drafting Brush 13
Ruling Pen 14
Rapidograph Pens 15
Lettering Guide 16
'Become a Draftsman' Advertisement 17
T-square 18
Adjustable Head T-square 19
Parallel Bar 20
Drafting Machine 20
30-60 Fixed Triangle 21
Adjustable Triangle 22
Machined Compass, Pencil 23
Large Bow Compass, Pencil or Pen 23
Small Bow Compass, Pencil 24
Large Circle Template 24
Timely Template 25
Plumbing Template 25

French Curve	26
Engineer's Triangular Scale, Architect's Flat Scale	27
Table of Scales Provided on Standard Scale Tools	28, 29
Albrecht Dürer Reproduction	31
Calcomp Plotter, ca. 1966	33
IBM PC, ca. 1985	34
Calcomp Plotter, ca. 1980	35
Oce TDS 600 Plotter, ca. 2010	36
Oce TDS Scanner, ca. 2010	37
The Chicago Cut—cutting a drawing-sized sheet from a roll	44
IBM Selectric Typewriter	46
Kodachrome slide	49
Ektachrome slide	49
Kodak Cavalcade Projector, ca. 1955	49
Kodak Carousel Projector, ca. 1990	50
Carousel Slide Tray Storage Box	50
Kresge Auditorium, Yale University, 1955. Eero Saarinen, architect	52
Study Model with Chip Board Contours and Foam Buildings	53
Hot Wire Cutter	53
Drawings in Tube Files	61
Tracings Stored in Tubes in Vault	61
Specifications Stored on Shelves in Vault.	62
Drawing Storage in Flat Files	63
Project Files in Stacked Boxes	64
Local Area Network Server	64
Archive in Bound Book Format	66
Bauhaus, Dessau, Germany, 1926. Walter Gropius, architect	69
Villa Savoye, Poissy, 1931. Le Corbusier, architect	69
Farnsworth Residence, Plano, Illinois, 1951. Ludwig Mies van der Rohe, architect	70
Northwestern Life Insurance Building, Minneapolis, 1964. Minoru Yamasaki	71
Falling Water, Mill Run, Pennsylvania, 1937. Frank Lloyd Wright	71
Richards Medical Research Laboratories, Philadelphia, 1960. Louis I. Kahn, architect	72
Vanna Venturi House, Philadelphia, 1964. Robert Venturi, architect	73
Portland Municipal Services Building, 1982. Michael Graves, architect	74
Habitat, Montreal, 1967. Moshe Safdie, architect	75
Walt Disney Concert Hall, Los Angeles, 2003. Frank Gehry, architect	76
Signature Towers, Dubai, proposed. Zaha Hadid, architect	78

Introduction

A graying man in white shirt, necktie and lap apron, perched on a wooden stool, hunches over a drawing board; his calloused graphite-stained fingers sharpen a pencil while checking the dimensions of a beam in a steel manual. A young woman with open collar and blue jeans, sitting in an Aeron chair, scrolls through a website on a huge monitor for an AutoCAD detail of a product to download into a CAD drawing, while talking on the phone.

Both work in an architect's office.

I know the graying man. I worked in architect's offices when he did. I still work in one. I know the young woman, too. They illustrate the span of an era of architectural practice that began after World War II and continues today.

My career in architecture began in September 1950 when I enrolled as a freshman at the University of Minnesota (UM). Until a few months before, an architectural career was not my intent. If anything, it would be music. The only knowledge I had about the field had come from preparing a report for career day in one of my high school classes. For some reason, maybe clairvoyant, I looked up architects and learned they designed buildings from the inside out, not outside in. Not much information for selecting a career. But I didn't know much about music, either.

The decision came from memorable advice from my new brother in law: "Go into something with a future. You can draw. Go into architecture". The simple statement carried the wisdom of a 25 year-old. It stuck.

Attending the University of Minnesota was easy in 1950. The streetcar commute from south Minneapolis was routine. Tuition was $65 a quarter. The architecture program was 5 years; design studio began on the first day.

Architecture was a department of the Institute of Technology (IT), the engineering school. It was housed in the top two floors of the Main Engineering Building. Architects and engineers shared a few basic courses. English was one. Derisively called "Engineering English" by liberal arts majors, it was actually an excellent foundation for learning clear and purposeful writing. College Algebra and other freshman math courses were shared. And of course Engineering Drawing.

Engineering Drawing provided the serious immersion to drafting that a similar course in high school had lacked. My high school drafting teacher did double duty as an assistant football coach. His interest in drafting was secondary. Instead of T-square and lettering drills, Mitch (Mr. Mitchell) introduced us to the pencil sketches of some of the best architectural renderers of the twenties and thirties. From his collection of reproductions we practiced the techniques and learned the appeal of broad stroke pencil sketching.

The college course ignored that nonsense and taught basic drafting skills: T-squares and triangles, lettering guides, manila paper, and 4H pencils. The teacher was strict about line weight, intersections, sheet organization, and lettering. I learned how drafting should be done. Except lettering. It was not possible for me to letter well using a pointed hard lead that we called a nail set.

Drawing and sketching courses came as electives. The teachers were from the art department, so the subjects included still lifes and models, not buildings. Media included pencil, ink, and watercolor.

I took art department courses in oil painting. The teacher, Walter Quirt, brought abstract expressionist approaches. His work and teaching clarified how feelings spontaneously emerge from an emotionally prepared person and become visually expressed. In his work, and in our student work, the expression was color on canvas. Thought intervened later. Art came from life. The approach was closely akin to Asian sumi-e (ink wash) painting, improvisational jazz, stream-of-consciousness writing, and, I learned later, the work of Louis I. Kahn.

Architectural design studio was the major course in all of the five years. Labs were scheduled 3 afternoons a week in the early years, increasing to 5 in fourth and fifth year. The studios were open all the time, so they were used as "home room". My drawing board was the place I stored my bag lunch and books when I arrived in the morning, and did math homework.

The object of architecture studio was design. Every assignment in every year, with the exception of the first quarter of the first year, was an architectural design problem. (Actually, some of us first year students expected even the beginning basic design exercises to be architectural. One was heard to comment across the room of 90, after a critic advised his solution was too architectural, "What the hell are we studying? Trombone playing?")

Project submissions were drawings. Media was pencil and ink on illustration board. Subjects were chosen based on the studio year. Second year students, for example, were assigned projects with a certain level of complexity and were expected to respond with a certain level of competence. The measuring system was based on the experience of the faculty team assigned to the studio. For major projects and end-of-quarter assessments a jury was assembled from the faculty and from architects in Minneapolis and St. Paul.

Faculty was a combination of career teachers and practicing architects. Young and not so young. Educated in the Beaux Arts tradition or the Bauhaus method. It was a good mix. It provided a broad range of viewpoints and values. Architecture is as much of a human study as a discipline.

Following graduation, I served two years in the Army Corps of Engineers during the early post-war period in Korea. My platoon built buildings and bridges and blew things up – construction work. On return I worked for architectural firms in Minneapolis and St. Paul and got architectural registration in Minnesota. Academia beckoned, and I enrolled in Lou Kahn's Master's program at the University of Pennsylvania.

The experience at Penn was life-forming. The exposure to Kahn satisfied my need to blend problem solving with purpose. The architectural design approach I had learned and practiced seemed superficial: follow the "rules" of Modern, pattern a good-looking façade and get published in the architectural press. Kahn taught how to search for the fundamental purpose of the project, understand its meaning. Every commission was unique, learning from the lessons of the previous. And from history.

Wanting to continue in academia after graduation, I looked for and found a teaching opportunity at Clemson University. My former teacher at UM, Harlan McClure, had become dean in 1954 and was building an excellent program. I stayed for 6 years. The time spent teaching with him was a valuable experience.

Architectural education evolved in the last 60 years just as, or perhaps because of, changes in architectural practice. Clemson initiated, in 1968, the change from a 5-year to a 4+2 year program for architecture. It was early in the trend that today is the standard for architecture programs. Concurrently, academic architecture programs became liberal arts studies as much as, or even more than, disciplines for practice.

Practitioners fuss about this trend. They complain that fresh graduates can't draw, don't understand building construction, and are not willing to spend a few years detailing toilets (like they did). That may be true, but they find that the new interns are just as motivated to learn the practice and quickly become adept at drawing and construction. They also bring new ideas.

My latest 40 years have been in practice with a firm in Jacksonville, Florida. KBJ Architects was founded in 1946 by three army veterans, Bill Kemp, Frank Bunch, and Bill Jackson. It is a medium-sized firm with a diverse practice of projects large and small, including schools, high rise offices, airport terminals, hotels, and churches. The tools and practices in the book have all been observed at KBJ in one form or another.

This background sketch is meant to provide a flavor to my involvement in the profession. Architectural practice is influenced by history, society, and the marketplace, but perhaps more by the education and experience of its practitioners.

Through all of the early moves and experiences, my wife Reagan was supportive and encouraging. Her lifetime of dedication is invaluable. Our sons, Richard and John, both architects, keep me in touch with today's issues and values. They offered sharp insight to the manuscript as it developed.

Attributions are used where academically appropriate. Much of the outside research was done the easy way: google the term and select the Wikipedia entry.

The sketches were drawn with 0.5 mm high polymer B lead on polyester film. The pencil was my favorite Pentel Twist Erase. Sketching was the best way to provide consistent illustrations of the key subjects. It helped me to understand the form and construction of each object, even familiar ones. Like all hand sketching, the process was a path into the mind of the designer.

Past tense is used as much as possible in the text, although some practices are difficult to think of as past since they are still in use. When in doubt, a point of view from 20 years hence was used, but strict adherence even to that was difficult. Forgive an occasional lapse into present tense. The idea should carry.

At this end of my career, the period of this writing, I see big changes from the other. Some of them are a natural evolution brought from gradual developments in technology, methodology, and society. Changes in architectural practices have been gradual – an evolution. Changes in the tools used to produce designs came suddenly in the 1990s with the introduction of computer aided design (CAD). That was more of a revolution. The tools became obsolete. Work moved off the boards.

The book is intended to provide a record of the tools and practices of that era. Like a rear view mirror in a car, it provides a reference to the road behind while we speed into the future.

The image of the man on the stool is only a memory. His era provided significant contributions to the practice of architecture. The tools and practices of that time will not be forgotten.

Chapter One: Boards

Conception easel.
Ideas hatch in its nest.
Architecture born.

A drawing board was the fundamental tool of the architectural design process. All the other tools—pencils, paper, T-squares—were brought to it. Although concepts may be drawn on the proverbial "back of a napkin" in a restaurant, serious development of those ideas was done on a drawing board. The "board" was the architect's home. Used for both designing and drafting, it defined the practice.

Most drawing boards available before WW II were made of white pine boards glued to form the desired size ("board" has a double meaning for both the individual components and the resulting table top). Typically the width was 36 to 38 inches and the length was 48 to 60 inches. As the supply of white pine became scarce, basswood became the standard.

Basswood offered advantages over pine in its lighter weight and finer, softer grain. Where basswood strips formed the main part of the board, hardwood was used for the side edges to provide a more durable guide for the T-square. The resulting board, whether made of white pine or basswood, was strong and stable. A good one lasted a lifetime.

To make the surface acceptable for drawing on thin tracing paper, the board was covered with enameled paper ("eye-ease" green on one side, buff colored on the other), stretched to fit tightly. The cover had to be periodically replaced, a task that required a few hours and best started near the end of the day so the paper could dry overnight. The paper was cut to fit around all four edges of the board, then thoroughly wet using a sponge or paper towel. Wrapping around the edges required making box pleats, like wrapping a gift. It was held in place on the back of the board with staples or with wide paper tape, which was also wet to activate the glue.

The process was much like stretching water color paper. Care and skill were required to assure no wrinkles at the corners or especially at the T-square edge. If the paper was too wet it would shrink too much, warp the board and produce a drum head. A fresh, successfully stretched board cover provided a moment of satisfaction—a moment that lasted until the first compass point or thumbtack hole was poked.

Drawings were held in place with thumbtacks, of all things. Thumbtacks were the enemy of the board, let alone the board cover and the drawing, since they pierced not only the cover but the basswood itself. Thumb tacks designed specifically for drafting had very flat heads and short tacks (to minimize damage to the board). Most drafters probably used "dime store" tacks, however. "Tack lifters", metal probes that allowed gentle removal of the tacks, preserved the fingernails.

One of the advantages of relatively soft basswood, as opposed to hardwood, was its ability to accept and hold a thumb tack. Varnished maple or other close-grained hardwood would have made a good drawing surface without the use of a board cover, but the drawing would have been held some other way, since thumbtacks were not as easy to insert into hardwood.

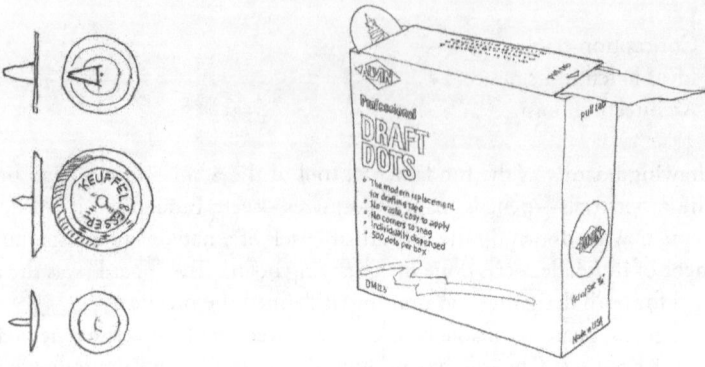

K+E Thumbtacks   **Drafting Dots**

Drafting tape was a welcome replacement to tacks. Its main disadvantage was its tendency to roll up when the T-square or parallel bar slid over, sometimes getting stuck on its underside. Usually the pieces could be reused a few times, but a large roll was required for frequent replacement. Masking tape was also used—a big roll was less expensive than drafting tape—but it lost its "stick" after one or two uses. Drafting dots replaced tape for those who could afford them. They were thinner, so roll-up was less of a problem.

Paper covers were replaced in the 60s by vinyl, a definite improvement. Vinyl not only did not need to be stretched, but offered a more supple base for pencil drawing. Thumb tacks were no longer an issue, but the occasional use of a compass point made a hole that healed itself. Vinyl also healed an occasional knife blade cut, but with too many cuts flaws would show up in the drawing.

The disadvantage of early vinyl was, in addition to the higher cost over paper, its difficulty of being cleaned. The recommended method for cleaning Borco brand board covers available in the 60s was to use lanolin, which in itself was hard to clean off. Later products cleaned well with mineral spirits.

With the introduction of vinyl covers, drawing boards could be made of almost any flat surface. Boards were produced with a particle board core, plastic laminate cover, and metal edges. An added vinyl cover made the surface suitable for quality pencil drafting, since the bare plastic laminate surface was too hard. Boards home-made of hollow core doors with a vinyl cover also made adequate boards. They were lighter weight and less expensive than either particleboard or basswood.

Work Stations

The standard architectural and engineering drafting room in the 50s was equipped with large wood drawing boards set onto metal or wood legs. Some of the board/table combinations were manufactured as a set, using hinges and support brackets so the top could have a variable tilt. Others were loose tops on separate tables, using wood blocks for the tilt.

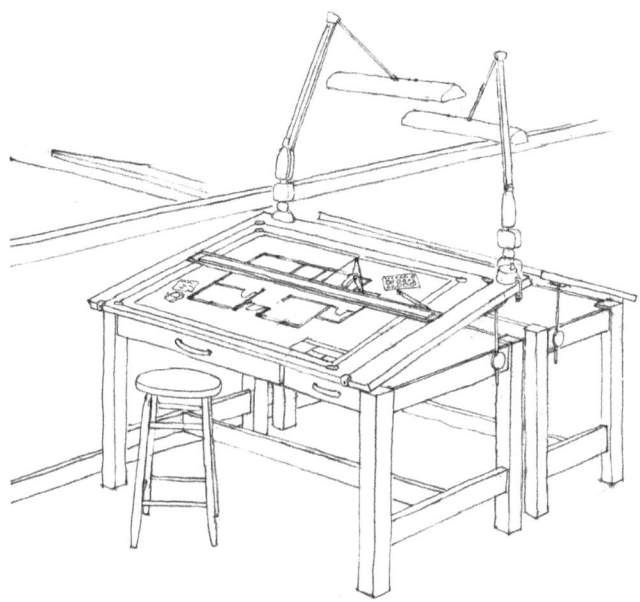

Work Station from the 1950s

In a typical drafting room up until the 1960s a work station was a single stand up drawing table with a stool. Several work stations were arranged side-by-side in rows, the length depending on the shape of the drafting room. Large offices had several rows and no walls or partitions between work stations. Some large offices (aka plan factories) arranged these "crank turner" desks around the perimeter, each facing the wall. The legend was the chief draftsman could sit in the middle of the room and demand to see only a-holes and elbows at work.

At the end of the day, tracings were returned to a plan file for safe-keeping. Personal supplies and tools were kept in a locked drawer at the desk. Drafters normally provided their own drawing instruments such as compasses and ruling pens, scales, leadholders, triangles, and T-squares. Parallel bars, replacing T-squares, were generally provided by the office, as well as expendable supplies of leads, paper, and erasers.

The design department, or studio, as the designers preferred to call it, was in a different section of the office or even in another room. Designers, either because of real need to see the bigger picture or simply for status, were the first group provided layout surface in addition to the drawing board.

Beginning in the 60s, stand up layout or reference tables were added for other work stations. With them also came privacy screens. Work stations were either "L" or "U" shaped, depending on the drafter's role in the office or project. Job captains, the drafters in charge of the working drawings for a project, warranted "U" shapes (drawing table either flanked by or tailed by 2 reference tables). Senior drafters got at least an "L" shape or shared a "U" with another. The size of the drafting room increased because of these new arrangements.

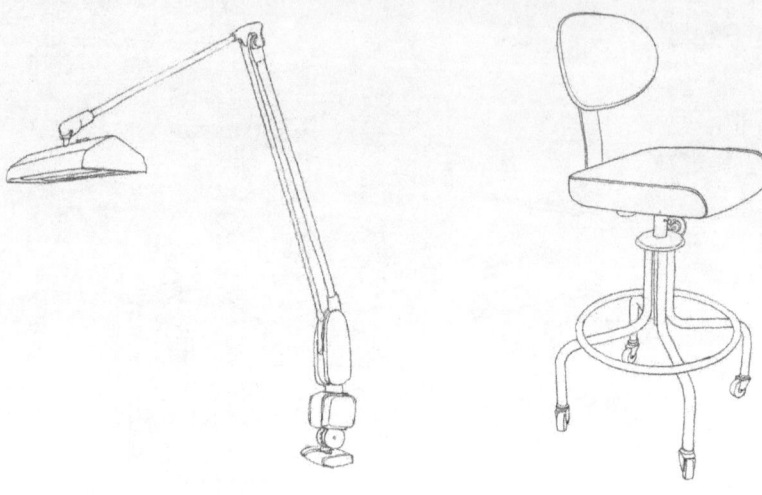

Dazor Lamp **Drafting Stool**

Project managers were housed in private or semi-private offices. The clerical staff worked in an office pool that looked much like the drafting room except with sit-down desks. Their work space furniture evolved much as that in the drafting room.

Lighting in the drafting room was generally poor in both quality and quantity in the 40s and 50s. Drafting stations were provided a Dazor brand desk light—a clamp-on fixture, copper/bronze color, with two 15-inch fluorescent lamps (whose ballast usually hummed). Room lighting evolved as it did in all office environments, becoming based on fluorescent luminaires following the trend to more and more foot candles.

As lighting consultants learned that quality of light was more effective than quantity, generalized room lighting was reduced and supplemented with task lighting. The task light evolved to an articulated arm desk light that used a combination circular fluorescent and incandescent lamp.

Another key factor in the evolution of the drafting room was the growth of telephone outlets. An early drafting room did not provide a phone for the drafters. Even the design studio had a common phone for all. Job captains were the first to get phones at their work stations so they could easily communicate with engineers and consultants in other offices.

Gradually phone outlets were extended to most and eventually to all work stations when it was recognized more employees needed to communicate with others outside of the office. Telephones became the primary means, at least before e-mail. Before long everyone had a telephone at their desk. Most offices, initially reluctant to provide phones for everyone, gave up trying to enforce telephone discipline to business calls only.

In the 1960s drafters realized that drawing board tables could be sit-down rather than stand-up. This became the source of controversy in many offices. Management felt that a policy had to be implemented for one or the other so the office would appear to be organized. Generally the challenge was between the "old-timers" and the younger architectural graduates, so it became not only an organizational question but a personal identity issue. Sit-down tables were considered to be more "professional"—more suited to the work space of a combination designer/project manager.

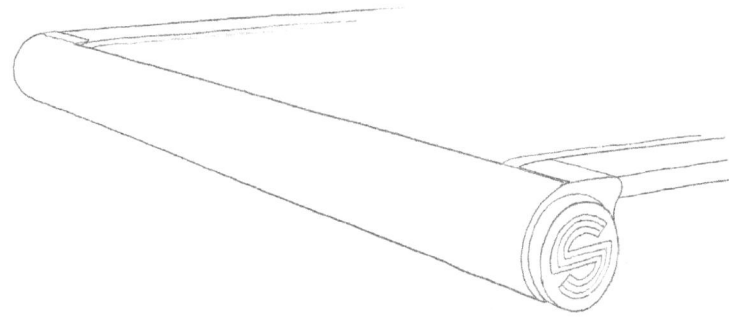

Spiroll Drawing Protector

Sit-down tables were made more comfortable for all day drafting with the development of the Spiroll. It was a metal sleeve into which the bottom of the drawing was rolled, protecting it while the upper part was worked on.

Eventually the "sit-downs" won, but "stand-ups" still had their advocates (remembering Thomas Jefferson's standup drawing table). For pure drafting, it was easier to see the entire drawing from a standing position. Ergonomically it was easier to get off of a stool rather than up from a chair when having to move around. The ideal set-up was a motorized version that traveled to all heights and angles, with an adjustable stool to match.

Stools evolved from simple wooden four-legged products to those with adjustable height steel frame, padded seats and backs, casters, and foot rings. They were replaced by chairs, which themselves evolved from simple task chairs to thousand-dollar ergonomic seating devices.

The change to CAD eliminated the primary purpose of the drawing board, whether stand up or sit down. Any that remained in a typical architectural office were holdovers used primarily for the large surface they provide for viewing reference drawings. The typical workstation remained "U" or "L" shaped, with the keyboard/monitor located in an intersection and the wings used mainly to lay out reference drawings.

Electronic drafting made drawing boards obsolete. Drawing boards live on only in memory and metaphor. People who have never even seen one understand what is meant by the statements "back to the drawing board" and "work on the boards". CAD moved the work off the boards.

Hand drawing, the work itself, evolved as well.

Chapter Two: Drawing

Imagination
Hiding in a graphite core,
Drawn out from a point.

Design requires the ability to visualize images. Images are drawn from the mind. Drawn, in this sense, means "pulling out" or lifting. We draw water from a well, blood from a vein, wire from molten metal, and occasionally we draw a lucky card.

An artist or an architect draws an image out of the mind and expresses it on paper. The physical record of this "drawing out" process is also called a drawing. There is a direct conduit from the mind through the hand through a tool that makes the drawing.

For some architects the favored tool was a pencil. Others relied on a marker pen. Some constructed study models. Some learned to use a computer to develop early concepts. More than one of these was used at different times for different purposes. The choice depended on the amount of control and feedback it provided. The tool also had direct influence on the design.

If we shape our tools and thereafter our tools shape us, to paraphrase Churchill, our drawing and design tools shape our architecture. Louis Sullivan's beautiful scrollwork designs would have been more static if they had been drawn with computer aided design (CAD) rather than freehand with a pencil. Lou Kahn's early training as a painter may have developed his sensitivity to architectural form revealed by light. Frank Gehry may not have even conceived of the shapes of Bilbao without knowing they could be drawn and built only with the aid of computers. Sigfried Giedion taught how the "discovery" of perspective drawing in 15th century Florence inspired designers to add depth to their facades.

Lego blocks, a toy beginning to be popular in the 60s, may have influenced the design of buildings. The references were evident in window glass flush with the exterior wall (like transparent Lego blocks combined with opaque) and "extruded" building shapes with mitered corners. Connection?

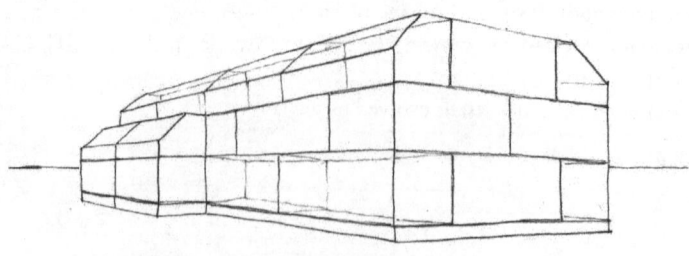

Lego blocks ca. 1970

Chapter Two: Drawing

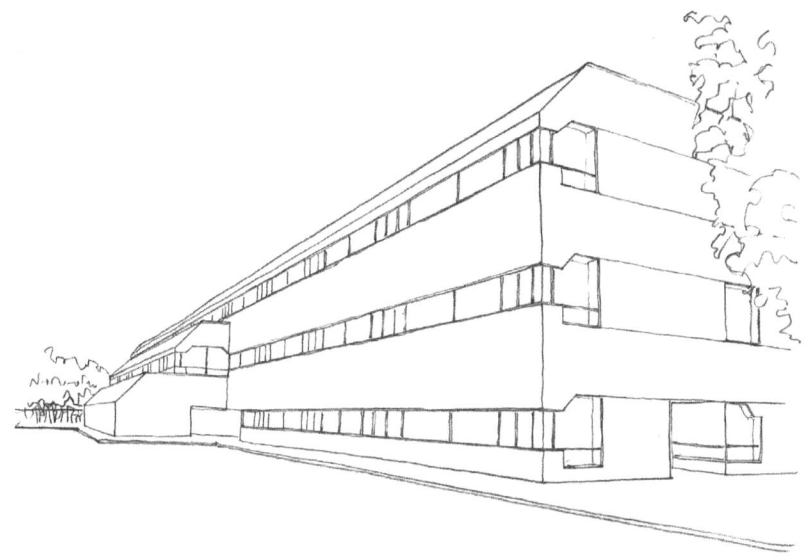

**Florida State College at Jacksonville, Downtown Campus, 1975.
RS&H Architects**

Pencils

Architectural and engineering draftsmen (later called drafters) drew with pencils, as they had for generations before. Pencil was a controllable medium that easily allowed trial and error development of an idea, quick views of the other side of an object, rendering and shading of form, and definition of major and minor elements by line weight. Ideas developed quickly through their use combined with tracing paper overlays. Changes were easily made by erasers. Pencil drawings were well suited to illustrate the design to others.

Wood pencils with graphite/clay "leads" have been around so long they are ubiquitous. Staedtler Mars in Germany recently celebrated the 350th anniversary of their earliest antecedent, vying with their Nuremburg neighbor Faber Castell for the claim of world's oldest pencil manufacturer.

Graphite pencil lead, especially softer formulations like 2B and 4B, produced quality shades and shadows that gave life to orthographic views. Using the broad side of the lead, lines of various widths could be drawn. Washes could be formed of graphite dust (salvaged from the pencil pointer) applied with a tissue or cotton ball. A pencil rendering on tracing paper was easy to reproduce.

Eero Saarinen drew design concepts using soft pencil on tracing paper. Rendering masters like Hugh Ferriss and artists like Ted Kautzky produced memorable work with graphite pencils. Paul Rudolph, though probably more renowned for his ink renderings, produced beautiful pencil work. Lou Kahn used pencil a great deal, as well as ink and charcoal. So did Romaldo Giurgola.

Mechanical drawing, or drafting, was a curricula course for architects and engineers through the 40s and 50s. Students learned how to use the tools, how the basic views were constructed and used, and proper lettering. The courses were dropped from the architectural curricula in the 60s. Drafting skills were expected to have been learned in secondary school or picked up in the course of design studio work. The expectation proved more or less correct. Drafting courses were tedious to future architects who wanted to create grand ideas. They learned to draw in the process.

Their primary tool was a pencil, and the pencils were often wood. To prepare a wood pencil for drafting, a correct point was required. Tools for this task included a sharp pocket knife, X-acto knife or single edged razor blade, and a sanding surface. The decision of how much lead to expose was determined by the drafting task—a lot, if the point had to be long for precise drafting with hard lead, but too long and the lead would break under pressure. If too short the cutting had to be repeated often.

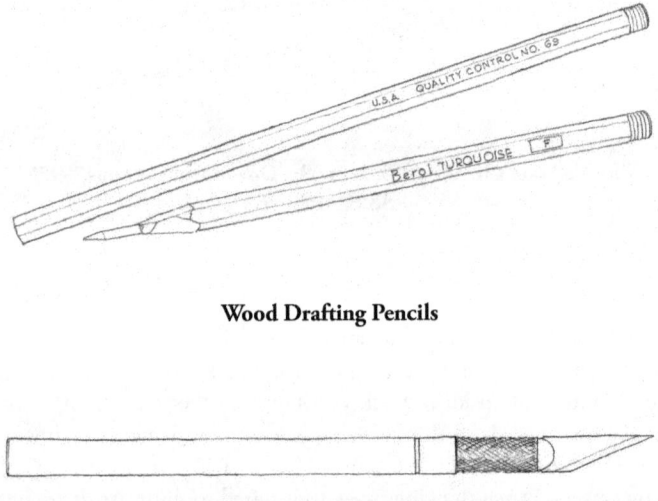

Wood Drafting Pencils

X-acto Knife with No. 11 Blade

The shavings were carefully dropped directly into a waste basket or simply onto the floor. That later became an unacceptable practice, but then the shavings just joined the ashes and butts of the cigarettes most draftsmen smoked at the desk. Another unacceptable practice. Wood or linoleum floors allowed for easy, it was thought, sweep-up by the custodians.

Pencil sharpeners of the crank kind that cut only the wood became available. This should have speeded the process, but usually the sharpener was across the room, taking time and effort to go to it. The hand-shaving process, although it took longer and was not as precise, allowed the drafter to stay at the desk and think about the next line to be drawn (or where to go for lunch) while methodically preparing his pencil. The drafting room's shared sharpener, on the other hand, allowed for socializing.

The final point was sanded to shape. Sandpaper, approximately 1 x 3 inches, was stacked on a board shaped to form a handle. The primary issue with using sanding blocks, as they were called, was how to make a perfectly symmetrical point. If the point was off-center, the line it drew would have a slight wave, since the pencil was rolled between the thumb and forefinger as it was drawn. Sanding blocks also allowed chisel points to be prepared for lettering.

Sanding Block

Secondary issues with a sanding block were where to store it and what to do with the graphite. The handle had a hole that allowed it to be hung on a string or hook from the edge of the desk. The loose graphite could then join the pencil shavings and ashes on the floor. Graphite was wiped from the pencil tip with a cloth or tissue, carefully directing it away from the drawing and keeping it off the fingers. The drafter examined the point for quality.

For really fine lines drawn with a 2H or harder, the point would then be "sanded" on a hard paper and then "tempered" by pressing and drilling it into a hardwood surface. This process that may or may not have had a scientific basis, but seemed to work.

During the 50s mechanical leadholders using 2 mm leads replaced wood pencils without much debate. Some holdouts insisted wood pencils were better—better "feel"; balance, touch, and control. They also missed the scent of the Cedar used in wood pencils. Eventually they all switched.

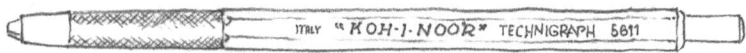

Leadholder

Given the variety of different leadholders available, the selection of leadholder depended on the drafter's hand size and shape, and personality. They each had their favorites and owned several different leadholders for different drafting tasks. One was assigned to each lead hardness currently in use, since it was easier to identify the lead type on the holder than on the lead itself.

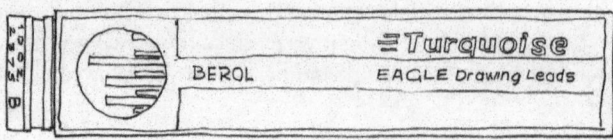

Package of B Leads

Lead pointer devices replaced sanding blocks. Though they had the same issues of where to store them and what to do with the graphite, their design and shape allowed them to easily produce a symmetrical point. The foam stabber ring pretty well settled the graphite issue, but there were other problems.

The most commonly used pointer type was the "pot". Made of heavy cast metal, it was supposed to stay in place on the desk while rotating the pencil. The weight was intended to allow a one-handed operation that avoided having to touch the graphite-smeared exterior with the other. It seldom stayed in place by itself and a slight off-center spin would break off the lead inside the pot. A desk clamp solved the stay-in-place problem, but that complicated the process of removing it for emptying.

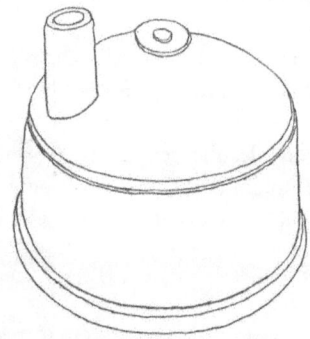

Pot Style Lead Pointer

Another issue with the pot was replacing the sandpaper unit; a truncated cone adhered to the inside of the pot. It was difficult to remove and was an extremely messy process. One benefit of the pot was that the graphite could be collected for use as washes on presentation drawings.

Other lead pointers were smaller. The pointing process was achieved by twirling the pencil with the fingers, rather than the forearm, like the pot. Some were attachments to electric erasers, piggy backing on the motor.

According to current drafting supply catalogs, these are still the tools available for pointing. Products currently produced must have made improvements, though. Right?

If a comparison was made of the economics of wood pencils/sanding blocks to leadholders/pointers, the factors included the first cost of each product and the time saved or expended in their use. It was doubtful there was any difference in time spent preparing and drawing, so the analysis focused on the cost of the products and their maintenance. Speculatively the lowest capital cost would be if both were used; wood pencils supplemented by a leadholder in the following way: a drafter used a wood pencil until it became too short to hold, then inserted the stub into a pencil extender until it became too short to sharpen, then peeled off the wood and inserted the lead into a leadholder, thus using all but about 1/2 inch of the graphite.

Graphite/clay (or graphite/polymer) leads applied smoothly on polyester (Mylar) drafting film. The lines flowed out of the point almost like ink from a brush. But they easily smudged. "Plastic" leads were developed especially for the film medium. They were generally the same size and shape as graphite leads but with different grade designations. Although their waxy feel was not as responsive as graphite, plastic had an advantage when used on film in that it bonded with the surface and became relatively smudgeless.

To alleviate the chore of pointing the lead, drafters looked for thin leads. Mechanical pencils like Eversharp had been available in the first half of the 20th century as general purpose writing instruments, but not for technical uses. Drafting-quality versions were developed in the 80s that used thin hi-polymer leads of constant diameters, like 0.5 mm, 0.7 mm, and 0.9 mm, that didn't need to be pointed. They were not adapted to drafting uses until after most architectural and engineering firms had converted to CAD, so their success for hand drafting was not measured.

Constant diameter soft leads were well suited for lettering and sketching. The most useful leadholders were those that provided a good grip and a long eraser that twisted into the barrel, making an all-in-one writing/drawing/erasing tool that eliminated the need for a pointer. Way to go, Pentel!

When color was desired it was usually applied to reproductions of drawings that had

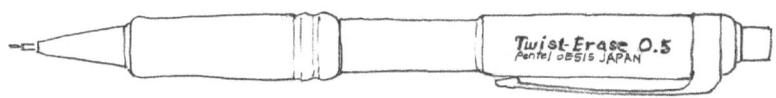

Pentel Twist Erase with 0.5 mm Lead

been hand drawn by graphite pencil or ink. Color was applied with colored pencils, which worked well for lines, trees, and details. Colored pencils were generally as easy to use and control as graphite leads, although more difficult to erase. One of the lines of pencils, Prismacolor, was available individually or (like Crayola crayons) in sets of 8, 12, 36, and up to 132 colors. Frank Lloyd Wright drew many of his designs with colored pencils.

For larger images water-color washes were applied with brush. Such washes, a specialty of the Beaux Arts era, allowed transparent shadows and gradations of surface form. Designers and students skilled with applying washes probably increased the amount of sensual curved and undulating surfaces in their designs since they could render them so well.

Brush-applied washes were replaced with felt-tipped marker pens. Prismacolor and Chartpak brands both provided complete choices of colors, and became the standard for both architects and artists.

Erasing

The disadvantage of pencil drafting, that it was not permanent, was countered by its benefit of being not permanent—erasable so changes may be made. Erasing had its own requirements for choice of product and skill of erasing method. The most-used products were Pink Pearl and Magic Rub. Basic types were either hand-held or electric operated.

Magic Rub eraser

Pink Pearl eraser

Hand-held erasers approximately 1 x 2 x 3/8 inches were used to erase both large areas of a drawing or single lines with the use of an erasing shield. The original types were rubber based for pencil lines. For ink lines, grit was added to the formulation. One brand had both; one type at each end. For pencil lines, skill was needed to remove the entire mark, avoid smudging, and avoid marring the surface of the paper. Ink removal required additional skill, but some abrasion of the surface was hard to avoid. A knife blade to scrape off stubborn ink was an essential tool.

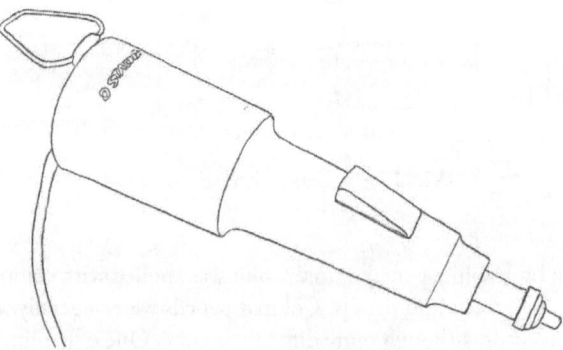

Electric Eraser

Electric erasing machines shaped like an in-line drill used an eraser insert about the same size and shape as a pencil. The eraser stick was held in place by a chuck. Electricity was supplied by either a battery or, more commonly, a power cord. Later versions included electric lead pointers as add-ons. The device came with its own issues such as where to plug it in, how to manage the cord, and where to set it when not in use.

Most erasing machines were heavy and cumbersome, out of scale with other more delicate drafting instruments. Their ability to erase with minimal arm movements (elbow grease) was offset by the effort to hold their top-heavy weight.

Erasing machines had their devotees. Some drafters considered owning one was a symbol of their professionalism. One of the most expensive drafting tools owned by the drafter, it traveled with from job to job.

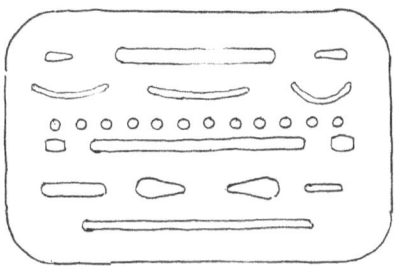

Erasing Shield

An erasing shield was a thin metal plate approximately 2 x 4 inches with cutouts of several sizes and shapes. It allowed a thin line to be isolated and erased by protecting the area surrounding the line. This also limited the amount of eraser crumbs and contributed to keeping the drawing clean.

Drafting Brush

Eraser crumbs were swept to the floor like all of the other debris that had to be removed from the table. A drafting brush's long horsehair bristles were very effective at removing eraser crumbs and overnight dust, without smearing the drawing.

The other product swept to the floor was used dry cleaner powder called Pounce. Packaged in a small pillow-shaped bag, it was sprinkled over the drawing to absorb excess graphite. As the T-square and triangles slid over, the powder would provide lubrication and separation from the drawing. Too much powder, of course, interfered with the drawing process, so the immediate area of work had to be swept clear with a brush.

Ruling Pens

> Precision machine.
> Sharp, black, confident wet line.
> Imprecise fingers.

A ruling pen, once used, was a tool that was hard to forget. Made with precision materials and machining, usually in Germany, ruling pens required more skill than the average or even the better drafter could provide. Much of that precision machining was lost in the application.

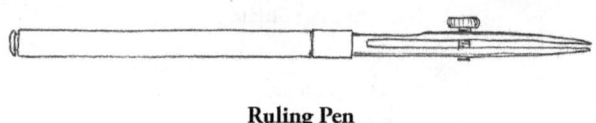

Ruling Pen

Architects who used ruling pens remembered the spilled India ink, hopefully not on the drawing. Remembered the chagrin when it was discovered that the new line did not match the width of the previous line, because the correct nib setting had not been reset after opening wider for cleaning. Or that the ink would not flow at all because the dried ink had not been cleaned off. The nibs would be either too dull or too sharp, or be worn into a blunt tip. Sometimes the ink got sucked under the edge of the triangle.

Even so, ruling pens were commonly used in the 19th and early 20th century. An architect drew the basics on paper with pencil; a skilled drafter traced the design onto linen with ruling pens. The entire design had to be laid out in pencil in sufficient detail to proceed to ink so it was, in effect, drawn twice.

The ink drafting process was planned in advance. While inking, each line had to dry before covering it with a T-square or triangle to guide the next line. If too much time was taken between lines, the ink in the pen would dry out. The nibs would have to be cleaned and refilled. Experienced drafters drew all the same width horizontal lines, starting at the top, then all the same width vertical lines, starting at the left. Then the nibs would be adjusted for the next width set and the process continued. All the short, partial lines that were missed were drawn later. Wait until all dried, then the pencil draft on the front and the ghost image on the back were removed with a soft eraser. Finally, the ink smears were scraped with an X-acto knife and the surface burnished so it could accept new lines.

India ink bottles were a problem in themselves. Some provided a metal "spoon" attached to the cap which could deposit a small drop of ink into the small crevice between the pen nibs. Or onto the drawing on the way over. A later improvement provided an eye-dropper attached to the cap. That should have simplified the delivery of ink, but the ink that clung to the outside of the dropper frequently smeared somewhere. When the bottle was nearly empty the dropper would become full of bubbles, which were hard to tell from real drops, so the ruling pen would appear full until a line was attempted to be drawn and the bubbles popped. Start again.

India ink lines were not only permanent, but looked good on paper, linen, or illustration board. Ingenuity led to the introduction of self-feeding technical pens. Rapidograph, a brand made by Koh-I-Noor, became common enough to have its name become generic. It featured a metal tube through which ink flowed. The diameter of the tube determined the width of the line. Ink delivery was controlled by a thin wire/stopper that rose up inside the tube to start the flow and dropped down to stop it. Ink was held in a reservoir in the barrel. Rapidographs were a vast improvement over ruling pens for their ability to draw lines, both ruled and freehand.

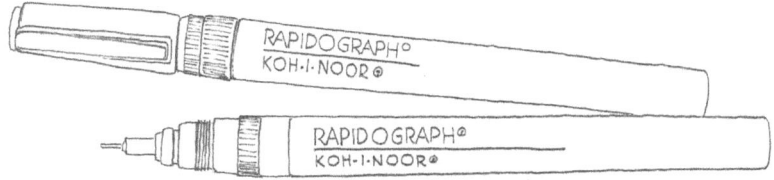

Rapidograph Pens

Even so, Rapidographs were not for everyone. Except with daily or frequent use, maintenance could require more time than was spent on production. A complete set of 6 to 8 pens of different widths was an investment that could be afforded by only those who used them a lot. The "office set" never seemed to get cleaned and usually the 0000 pen was missing. Mylar was especially hard on the tips—it wore out all but the expensive type. Even with those issues, they were a quality tool for the right application. They were an excellent tool for lettering.

Lettering

Lettering required special tools. A drawing that was primarily ink looked more professional if the lettering was also ink, but that task was not for a ruling pen. Before Rapidographs became available, tools used for free hand ink lettering included various shapes of brass nibs or quills that fitted into wooden shafts—tools that seemed straight from the 19th century. Their main advantage was that they were simple and direct—dipped into an ink pot and applied to the paper. Fountain pens used for handwriting would not perform with India ink.

Serious drafters lettered with plastic templates. Really dedicated ink drafters used Leroy lettering sets. Leroy is the brand name for a set of templates and styli developed for ink lettering by K+E (Kueffel and Esser) in the early part of the 20th century. The stylus operated like a pantograph—one leg riding in a template groove, the other applying ink. A complete set had several templates of various size letters, and styli of various width nibs. The nibs were similar to those in Rapidographs and carried similar issues of maintenance and expense.

Faster and more economical, freehand pencil lettering became predominant in architectural and engineering drafting rooms. Pencil lettering required a different technique than line work. Whereas for lines the pencil lead was uniformly pointed and relatively hard, for lettering the lead was softer and slightly chisel-pointed.

Not all drafters were proficient in quality lettering, as measured by uniformity of size, slant, readability, and spelling. Some offices assigned specialists to produce the door and finish schedule sheets, for example. Although a specialty, this was not a high-value assignment.

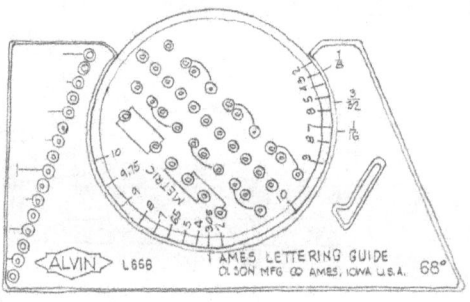

Lettering Guide

Uniformity of size and slant was aided by means of lettering guides. A guide was a clear plastic shape that contained holes for the pencil point to draw uniformly spaced guidelines. They were required to be used by students in their first drafting class. Some offices insisted they be used for all drawings, but experienced drafters could "eyeball" evenly spaced guidelines a lot faster without the guide.

Office standards dictated lettering standards for certain applications, including the size and slant of the letters. The reasoning for the slant was, since not all vertical strokes were truly vertical, and a backward slant appeared amateurish, it was better to have them all slanted forward a standard amount. Although not always uniformly slanted, even from the same drafter, deviations were less objectionable than for vertical letters. Offices that took pride in their work looked to the appearance of their drawings, including the lettering, as a critical measure of quality.

Drawing and drafting

There was something in the process of hand drawing—a pencil drawing (the verb) across a paper surface to produce a drawing (the noun)—that either required, or brought out, the understanding of the nature of the objects being represented. It also revealed the thinking process of the drawer. The future potential of job applicants' abilities could be predicted simply by reviewing the quality of drafting in their portfolio. Employers claimed that drafting could also reveal attributes like attitude and aptitude, even with beginning drafters.

The men and women who used the tools from the hand drafting era seemed to know how to think clearly and to understand how to put buildings together. Maybe they naturally understood the process. Maybe they learned it from their tools.

Drafting is a subset of drawing. A line drawing may be composed of either freehand or ruled lines; drafting defines a line drawing constructed with straightedges to a measurable scale. Edge-guiding tools were selected with care.

Adapted by the author from an advertisement for a correspondence course at The American School, Chicago, c. 1937

Chapter Three: Edges

Stands at attention,
Assuring edges ready.
Unwavering line.

Edges guided the pencil or pen in straight or curved lines. The lines were vertical or horizontal relative to the sides of the paper—orthogonal. T-squares and 90 degree triangles were the primary tools for straight orthogonal lines. Compasses and plastic templates of various shapes were used for the curves.

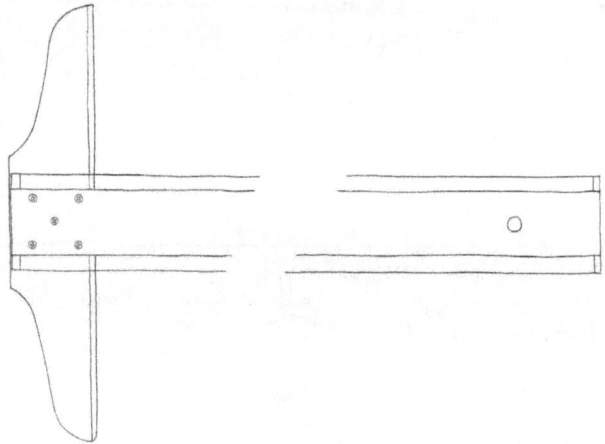

T-square

T-Square

T-squares were used for as long as drafting had been done, perhaps several hundred years, and became legendary as the common tool for architects. Architects in Philadelphia organized themselves into the "T-Square Society" in the 19th century. Frank Lloyd Wright revealed in his Autobiography the story of a T-square fight in Louis Sullivan's drafting room in the late 19th century (probably a disagreement involving architectural integrity).

It was a simple tool (or weapon). Most were made of hardwood with plastic upper and lower edges. The plastic edge strips were not as thick as the wood stem. The resulting gap broke the capillary that would otherwise suck ink under the edge. Since almost all drawing activity used the upper edge, sometimes the bottom edge was sacrificed for use as a cutting guide.

Adjustable head units were developed in the early part of the 20th century by K+E and others. They featured a second head mounted on the top of the stem above the fixed head. The tool was turned over and the head was adjusted to the new angle, allowing a setting for a series of lines at a slightly different angle than the factory setting. Architects usually found it easier to just realign the paper.

CHAPTER THREE: EDGES   19

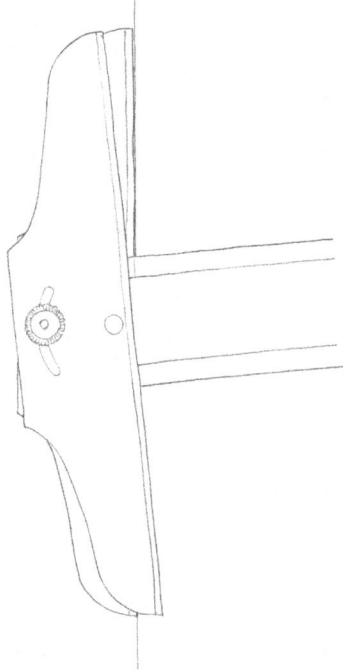

Adjustable Head T-square

The life span of the adjustable unit could be extended by turning it over when the upper edge became nicked from wear. The bottom edge became the new drawing guide (provided it had not been even more damaged from use as a cutting guide).

T-squares required training and experience to use, especially if more than 36" long. The left hand (for right-handed drafters) held the head tight against the left edge of the board while simultaneously guiding a triangle. When working at the far right side of the drawing, the left hand had to repeatedly check to maintain the head tight against the board edge. The board edge itself had to be maintained true and straight, with no dents or gouges.

One feature of the T-square was revealed as a benefit only after the parallel bar was introduced—the ease with which it could be removed from the board, allowing unfettered (no cables) access to the entire drawing table.

Parallel Bar

Parallel bars almost universally replaced T-squares in the 60s. The drafter held the bar in place with one hand without having to constantly keep it tight against the board edge, as with a T-square. Using parallel bars, multiple drafters could work on the same drawing from one day to the next, adjusting the alignment to yesterday's "hand."

Parallel bars were controlled by braided steel cables (fabric cords in some designs) mounted near the side and top edges of the drawing board. The cables traveled through the bar in an arrangement that allowed the bar to travel up and down the board without changing its angle or alignment. The alignment setting was adjusted by loosening the clamp that held the cable fixed. Some versions, used on portable boards, had grips or glides over the edges of the board instead of cables, much like a T-square with a head at each end.

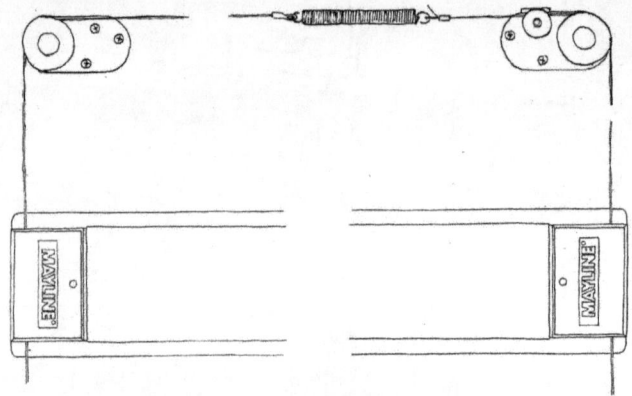

Parallel Bar

Bars 48 inches long or longer could be counted on to hold alignment, so sheet sizes grew to 42 or even 48 inches wide. An even longer bar allowed the side cables to be located even further apart, providing more uncluttered space on the board.

There were two models of parallel bars: the basic was plain on the underside; the upgrade had small rollers that kept the bar slightly above the surface to reduce smearing the graphite. The rollerball type had a shallower grip (which was actually the housing for the cables), so the drafter's hand was closer to the drawing surface as it guided the pencil across. The disadvantage of the shallower grip was the bar had to be picked up with the extreme tips of the fingers, a difficulty that produced imaginative home-made devices to reduce finger-tip burn.

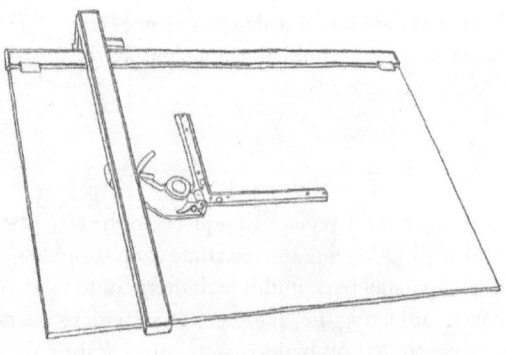

Drafting Machine

Drafting Machine

Drafting machines were developed in the first half of the 20th century. Used for guiding the pencil as well as providing a built-in measuring scale, they took the place of a T-square, triangle, and scale in a single unit. They were precision tools. Not "machines" in the usual sense, but "L" shaped rulers attached to a bracket that, wherever it was moved on the drawing, kept its alignment until changed by a wheel clamp device. The rulers were interchangeable for different scales and the brackets allowed the angles to be quickly adjustable. They were used mostly by industrial and civil engineers and surveyors who needed to draw short lines at many different angles. Architects seldom used them.

Triangles

Triangles, the companion piece to the T-square or parallel bar, came in several shapes and sizes but they all had one 90 degree angle. Most drafters used a minimum of two—45-45 and 30-60 degree shapes. Small (3 or 4 inch) triangles were also useful for drawing a series of short vertical lines.

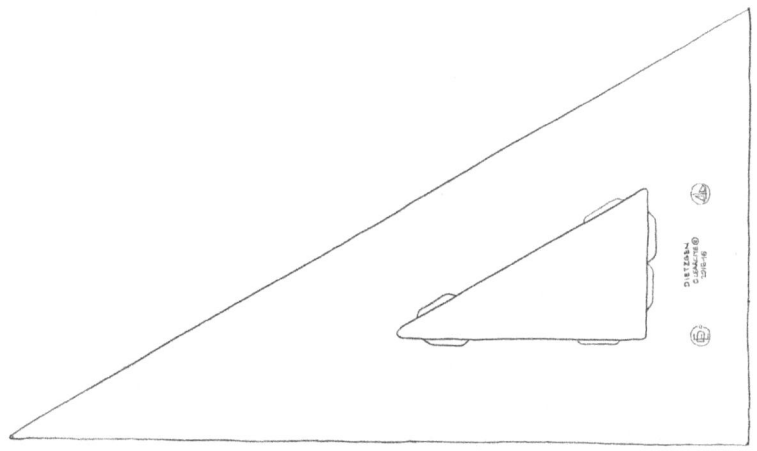

30-60 Fixed Triangle

An adjustable triangle, based on the 45 degree shape, could replace most of the other fixed sizes and angles. Since the practical size of an adjustable triangle as well as a fixed 45 degree unit was limited to 10 -12 inches (they took up too much space on the drawing), most drafters had a tall 30-60 triangle available for drawing long vertical lines.

Fixed triangles were not easy to pick up with one hand. Early versions were modified by drafters with pickup devices applied to the surface. Later models came with milled finger grips on the inner cut-out. The threaded knob that controlled the angle of an adjustable triangle made a good lifting grip.

Triangles, like all drawing tools, needed frequent cleaning since they picked up graphite from the drawing. Cleaning fixed triangles was easy—they could be held under the faucet, rubbed with soap, mineral spirits or other solvent, then dried with paper towels. Adjustable triangles required more deliberate cleaning. The traveling part had to be removed, and the crevice under the angle marker plate was hard to clean and dry. Solvent cleaners were not used because they softened the glue that held the plate. In all, adjustable triangles required more care, but their utility was worth the effort.

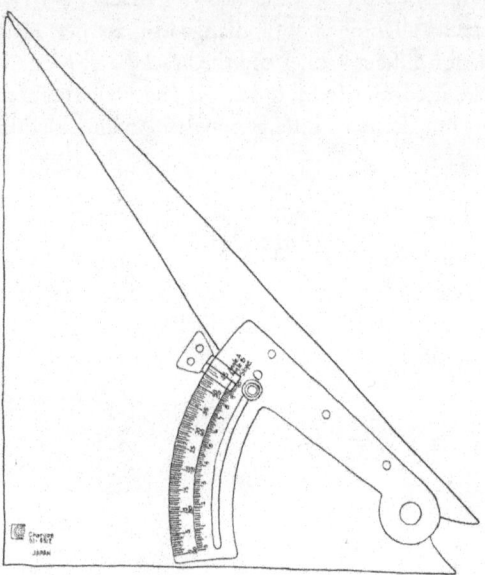

Adjustable Triangle

Some triangles, like T-squares, had edges that were milled to either a step or an angle to stand off slightly from the drawing. This feature was needed for ink ruling pen drawing, otherwise the ink could get sucked under the triangle. The gap from the raised step broke the capillary. Before milled-edge tools were available, drafters used home-made methods to raise the edge, like gluing pennies or acrylic discs to the underside.

Using a triangle for drawing, right-handed drafters laid the triangle point-right and drew, either top to bottom or bottom to top, against the left edge so the pencil angle could be controlled—the cross-handed method. For ruling pen work the line was drawn from the bottom up. Flipping the triangle to draw against the right edge was awkward, used only for lines on the extreme right side of the board.

Curves

Until plastic templates were available, curved lines of either ink or graphite were drawn with a compass. Ink compasses were tipped with the same nibs used on ruling pens, that difficult-to-master, hard-to-clean, blotch-making tool. They presented the same issues as ruling pens. Wide lines were not as difficult as narrow lines (the ink flowed better). Most curved lines, however, were secondary to the heavier profile lines and therefore narrow.

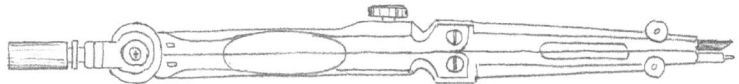

Machined Compass, Pencil

Using a compass to draw radiused filets, or rounded corners, entailed one of two methods. If the tangents had already been drawn, the center point of the arc was located by either geometric construction (miters, etc) or by measurement with a scale. Then the compass point was inserted precisely and a trial arc was drawn to assure it would meet the tangent points of the straight lines. The other method was to draw the arc first then the tangent lines. With ink drafting, the next issue was to set identical line widths on both the compass and the ruling pen used to draw the tangent lines. A precise match was not an easy task, given the infinitely adjustable nib-setting screws.

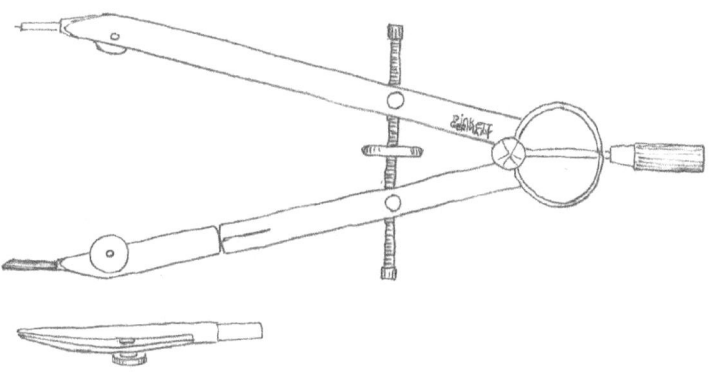

Large Bow Compass, Pencil or Pen

As frustrating as ink compasses were, pencil versions were not much better. The proper point was a chisel shape rather than a round one produced by a pointer. The chisel shape, especially with a soft lead, soon dulled, producing a fuzzy line that was not as precise as the tangent lines it connected. With a hard lead, pressure had to be applied directly onto the lead-holding arm of the compass. Small compasses that used a radius-setting wheel were fairly stable under pressure, but on larger versions with friction pivots, the arms stretched under pressure, distorting the radius. Pressure also gouged a big hole in the drawing.

Holes in the drawing (and the board) made by compass points were inevitable, but the damage could be mitigated. A "light touch" was best. If the lines had to be bolder than a light touch allowed, a couple of tools were available. One was provided in the drafting instrument kit, best described as a miniature table (approximately ½ inch diameter) with a clear plastic top and three extremely short pins for legs. The top had a dent in the center in which to set the compass point. The idea was that the pins provided stability without piercing the drawing.

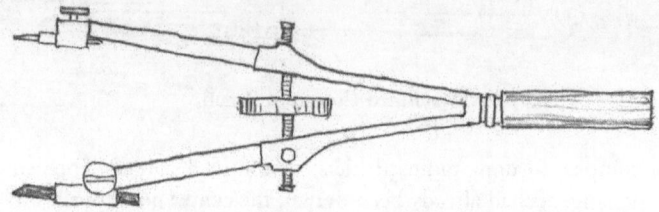

Small Bow Compass, Pencil

The other tool, more improvised, was a small piece of drafting tape set in place on the drawing and on which the radius center was marked. The tape absorbed most of the pierce of the compass point.

Curved lines were avoided (could it be that Modern Architecture was strictly orthogonal until circle templates were available?). Although the compass was not missed, it was actually the last tool to be discarded from the traditional set of machined drafting tools, outlasting the ruling pen and divider.

Circle templates, or circle makers, were instantly accepted and became as indispensable as triangles and T-squares. Plastic templates came in several sizes. The common version provided circles up to about 1½ inch diameter; larger templates up to 2 - 3 inches. They guided the pencil in a circle, in a curved line around a corner, or to describe the swing of a door. They were convenient for drawing circular symbols and grid bubbles. Specialty templates for shapes like toilet fixtures, ellipses, beam sections, and letters of the alphabet were available for drawing almost any shape.

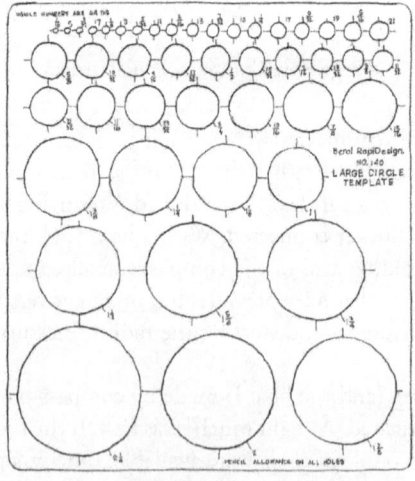

Large Circle Template

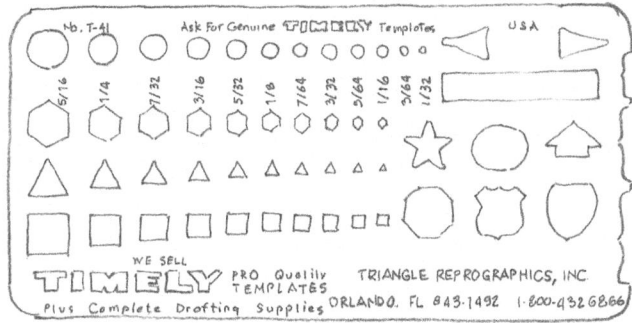

Timely Template

For curves larger than those a template could provide a variety of tools were available. Probably the best was a beam compass. Some compasses held a lead directly, but other versions held a complete pencil or lead holder. Pointing was easier, since the lead or pencil could be removed and sharpened in a pointer (by this time, drafters had given up trying to draw curved lines by using a chisel point). Even the simple elementary school compass was commonly used in the design studio, since it was precise enough for preliminary work, and allowed the use of colored pencils and felt tipped pens.

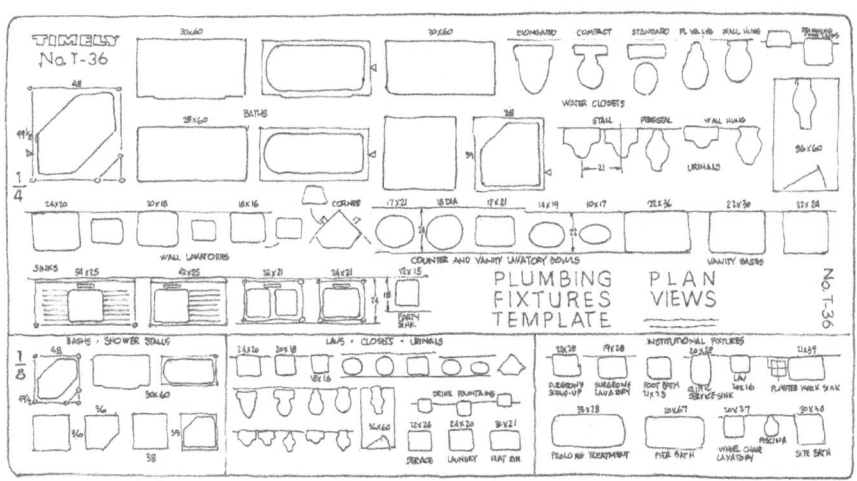

Plumbing Template

French curves of one or two shapes were in the tool kit of most architectural drafters but seldom used. Since building designs were required to be dimensioned, curves needed to be rational; a curve whose radius is constantly changing is not measurable by the typical architect or builder.

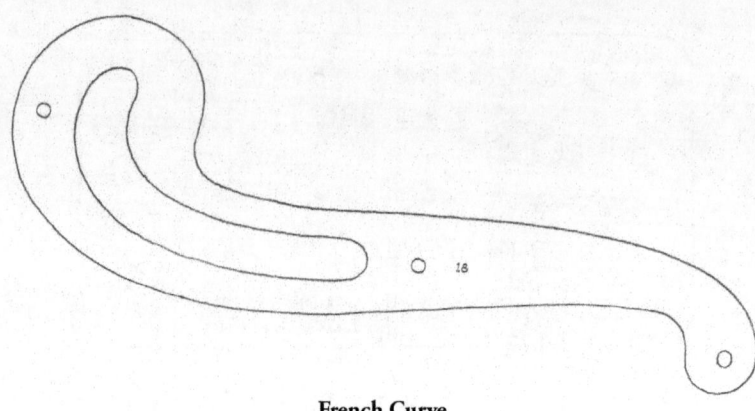

French Curve

Computers

Architects imagined that computers, when they arrived, would turn freehand sketches into straight and measurable lines overnight. All the tedious drafting would be avoided. A designer could sit in a comfortable chair and draw freehand on a computer screen with a light pen, rather than reaching over a large drawing board to draw small shapes in the upper corner.

Several prototype machines were imagined. With one, a sketch was inserted into a slot and came out a ruled drawing. With another, actually built, the drawing board was a digitizer tablet—everything drawn by hand was electronically recorded, straightened, then manipulated. A portable computer screen on which a person could draw with a stylus was also actually built. It not only straightened the lines but could also be used to digitize hand-written notes, thereby bypassing the typing process.

But the computers that were produced and used by architects operated differently than were imagined. They did come with a comfortable chair and they drew very straight lines, but instead of accepting a freehand sketch they required an image be constructed by inputting and connecting points—one after another after another. They encouraged repetition, mirroring, copying, classification, organization, and regularity.

Either architects did not convey their desires to the makers, or else computer designers did not understand the design thinking process of architects. Gestalt and binary math didn't seem to be compatible.

CAD is accepted today. Architects adapted their thinking to its nature. The design process evolved from hand drawing lines on paper to electronically digitizing points. The new lines are very straight and the measurements are extremely precise.

Chapter Four: Scales

Tiny numbered ticks.
Big ideas. Small drawing.
Miniature world.

Like so many terms in the building design field (building and design being two others), the word scale has more than one meaning. As an adjective it can refer to the relative size of an object. The statement, "this building has no scale", a comment heard even from learned critics, simply means there are no apparent scale-giving elements with which to determine size relative to people. Scale, as a verb, can refer to the act of measuring, as in "scale that drawing for me." A scale can also be a metaphor for the friendly rivalry between architects and engineers—an architect caught using an engineering scale is really slumming, and vice versa.

Scale the noun was a tool with measuring marks used for architectural and engineering drawing. Scales did not evolve much in the past many years. The primary changes were in how they were used. In hand drafting, a scale was integral with the drawing process; a drafter often had a pencil in the right hand and a scale in the left, setting the scale aside only when guiding the bar or the triangle. With CAD, if used at all, it was only to check a plot.

Architectural scales were one of two shapes—flat or triangular—whereas engineering scales were usually triangular. The measuring mark sets on scales (1/8" = 1'-0"; 1" = 100', etc) originated years earlier. The history of the origin of these scale groups would be an interesting study. Since both architect and engineering scales in America used feet and inches, the origin was probably linked to the Anglo-Saxon world.

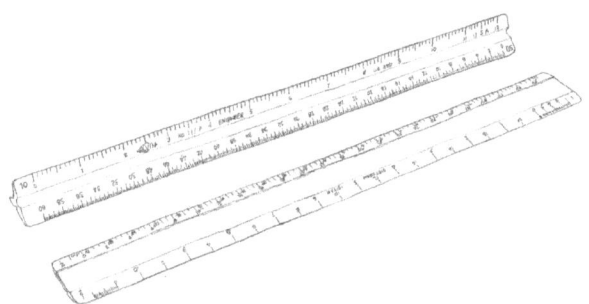

Engineer's Triangular Scale, Architect's Flat Scale

Feet and inches were called Imperial units (formerly called English units even though England used metric). Metric scales were called Standard International (SI) units. United States may be the only country in the world that still uses Imperial units.

Whether an architect used a flat or a triangular scale was a matter of personal preference. Triangular units offered a full scale ruler plus two more scales than flat—the seldom used 3/16" and 3/32". Flat scale users missed these options only when trying to measure a half-size plot of a 3/8" detail.

Much of the choice had to do with the peripheral uses for the tool. A triangular scale was useful as a guide when shearing a piece from a roll of tracing paper, but a flat scale could be used as well, in a different way (see "Chicago cut" described in the Documents chapter). A triangular scale was easier to hold steady when used as an expedient edge guide for drawing a straight line (a strict no-no in drafting class). A flat scale was somewhat easier to read from a lower angle of view, and a 6" long version could be carried in the shirt pocket.

When beginning a drawing by hand, one of the first decisions was what scale to use, determined by the purpose of the drawing, the size of the object, and the size of the paper. Architects selected a scale fraction based on even-numbered denominators like 1/8" = 1'-0", ½" = 1'-0", etc. Engineers preferred scales based on units of 10, such as 1" = 10'. 1" = 50', etc.

Both disciplines referred to Imperial drawing scales in common usage terms; for example 1/8" scale meant 1/8" = 1'-0" and 50th scale meant 1" = 50'. 1 to 50 or 1:50 meant 1" = 50" in both Imperial and metric.

The scales found on standard architect or engineer scale tools are listed in the chart. The Metric column indicates scales found on standard metric scale tools. No single tool had all the metrics; it required as many as to four to acquire all of them. The metric scales in bold were available on a single tool.

SCALES PROVIDED ON STANDARD SCALE TOOLS
Bold-face architect scales available on standard flat scales
Bold-faced metric scales preferred by PBS PQ260 MDG
(Figure Continued on pg. 29)

RATIO	ARCHITECT A" = 1'-0"	ENGINEER 1" = B'	METRIC
1:1	12"		
1:2			**X**
1:2.5			x
1:4	**3"**		
1:5			**X**
1:8	**1-1/2"**		
1:10			**X**
1:12	1"		
1:16	**3/4"**		
1:20			**X**
1:24	1/2"		
1:25			x
1:30			x

RATIO	ARCHITECT A" = 1'-0"	ENGINEER 1" = B'	METRIC
1:32	3/8"		
1:40			x
1:48	1/4"		
1:50			X
1:64	3/16"		
1:75			x
1:80			x
1:96	1/8"		
1:100			X
1:120		10'	
1:125			x
1:128	3/32"		
1:192	1/16"		
1:200			X
1:240		20'	
1:250			x
1:300			x
1:360		30'	
1:384	1/32"		
1:400			x
1:480		40'	
1:500			X
1:600		50'	
1:720		60'	
1:1000			X
1:1200		100'	

Metric

Metric was the standard in Europe for over 200 years. Its introduction in America was opposed by many, including Thomas Jefferson; he thought it was too artificial compared to the more anthropomorphic feet and inches. Its acceptance in America was a slow process.

In the 1980s the federal government installed a very ambitious program, outlined in the 1995 Metric Design Guide, with the goal of complete conversion to metric before 2000. All federal construction projects were required to be drawn in "hard" metric (no Imperial units allowed, even as duplicates). The government's position was that the only way to learn to use metric was to totally remove the Imperial equivalent, like the total immersion theory for learning a foreign language.

Several federal agencies (GSA, US Courts, military, etc), however, did not strive to enforce the goal, and each developed its own rules for metric application. Some required hard metric, some required both systems, and for some it was either optional or not preferred. State and local agencies had similar ambiguous guidelines.

Metric conversion hadn't really "taken hold" in daily living either. Most products on a store shelf were sized in metric. Shoppers began to accept the new units, but most gave up trying to figure out how much 750 ml of vodka was compared to a fifth (but then, how many remembered that a fifth referred to a fifth of a gallon?). They just bought the bottle on the shelf, suspecting "they" were changing the units in order to disguise another price increase.

More and more construction products became dimensioned in metric units. Product literature provided both SI and Imperial dimensions. Design professionals slowly learned to "think" in metric, at least for product dimensions if not so much for weights and volumes. For example, with objects sized in modular Imperial dimensions like 4, 12, and 24 inches it was relatively easy to remember the approximate metric equivalent 100, 300, and 600 millimeters.

As complicated as it was to convert the construction industry to metric, the challenge for land planning, surveying, and property records was even greater. Imagine converting every legal description archived in every title company to metric. Or every property record in every tax assessor's file, even if metric applied to only the horizontal dimensions of property.

For property surveys angles in metric were expressed in degrees with a base 360, the same as in the Imperial system. Angles could have been converted to decimal degrees in either SI or Imperial. Degrees and decimal fractions of degrees would be easier to handle. But surveyors traditionally recorded them in degrees, minutes, and seconds. Modern specialty calculators easily handled the arithmetic of subtracting 20 deg 42 min 13 sec from 119 deg, 2 min, 58 sec, but it was not easy by hand. Vertical ground elevations and horizontal distances were recorded in the same survey in feet and decimals of feet (and architects promptly converted them into feet and inches, for some reason).

Metric advocates claimed there were fewer units—millimeters (mm), centimeters (cm), decimeters (dm), meters (m), kilometers (km), to name a few—but that was more units, not less. The MDG eliminated all except millimeters. Millimeters was a convenient measure for small parts, but not for large.

The MDG made dimensions for large parts or for entire buildings more readable by specifying a gap to the left of xxx mm (for example 2 500 refers to two thousand five hundred mm). The guide did not indicate if dimensions for even small parts should display all those places (i.e. 0 010 for 10 mm), or if there would be a certain minimum size of object where the places rule changed.

Strict adherence to the MDG millimeter-only rule produced some awkward, hard to visualize, dimensions. For example, a building that was 10 265 mm long was read as ten thousand two hundred sixty five millimeters. It seemed more sensible to simply use a comma, or better yet to say it was 10.265 meters long.

The practice in the United Kingdom (UK) was to use meters rather than millimeters and therefore a decimal rather than a gap, to avoid misunderstanding (when was a gap just a typo?).

Life-long metric users learned to think in metric just as readily as their counterparts thought in feet and inches. Metric was simpler in many ways, including its ability to do arithmetic. It could benefit from adjustments, but improvements could have been made to the Imperial system as well.

Think how much simpler if inches were eliminated and small units were dimensioned in decimal fractions of feet. Yards would be discarded, like rods and chains were long ago. Miles can be kept—they were prevalent on the nation's highway signs.

Maybe it's too late to improve the Imperial-system world. Metric is here to stay. AEs, even those whose practice is strictly domestic, should learn this second language.

CAD Scale

The "tablet" on which an object was drawn in CAD was called model space. It represented 3 dimensions. One of the liberating aspects of CAD was that, in model space, the drawing's "field" was, in effect, limitless, like space itself. A line may be drawn in model space a hundred miles long and high without running out of "paper". Or a thousandth of an inch long and still be visible.

This amazing feature of CAD was metaphysical: space (or a computerized model of space) existed before an object was drawn—Newton's and Einstein's version of relational

Albrecht Dürer, *Draughtsman Making a Perspective Drawing of a Woman* (1525).
Metropolitan Museum of Art, N.Y.
Early Illustration of CAD Paper Space Viewport into Model Space

space. But then, if the space didn't really exist before an object was drawn—Descartes' premise that space required a physical object to give it meaning—what we saw was really only a blank screen. Either way, CAD provided three limitless dimensions hiding in a box.

Another element of experience with CAD was its ability to zoom into and out of the drawing, the space. Quite a different point of view than provided by a blank sheet of paper.

CAD was scale-less. The drawing was scaled in the sense that it had a size relative to the screen; scale-less in the sense that it was drawn full size. Objects were drawn "full size" with three dimensions on x, y, and z planes. For example, a door was drawn 3 feet wide by 7 feet tall by 1¾" thick, not scaled down as it would on paper. Generally, the z plane was kept at zero.

The operator worked with "real" dimensions. To determine the size of the object in the drawing, the command was called "Distance". "Dimension" was the command for annotating distance.

A dimensional protocol, either Imperial or metric (SI), was selected as one of only a few setup choices required to begin a CAD drawing. After that, scale was selected only for the plotting or publication of the drawing.

Plotting was the same as printing, except done on a plotter. Printing, the term usually applied for producing text documents on a printer, used the same technical process. The difference was in the size of the reproduction and the machine.

Before paper space was added to AutoCAD programs in the 90s, plotting was sourced from model space. A plan of a large building was split into sheet-sized portions and drawing titles and borders were drawn to a scale large enough to fit. For example, if the plan was to be plotted at 1/8" scale (1/8" = 1'-0"), the sheet was drawn 96 times full size. The plot command brought them all back to 1/8" scale.

Paper space provided the screen view that helped to convert a CAD drawing to paper. When in the paper space mode, the operator "punched a hole" (a viewport) in the screen, considering it an imaginary piece of paper, to reveal the underlying model space drawing. The image was selected, then enlarged or reduced to the selected scale for plotting.

Although a new and welcome innovation for CAD operators, the concept was understood by artists as early as the renaissance period.

Scale commands for a plot from model space used ratios like 1/96, rather than comparatives like 1/8" = 1'-0". From paper space, the Plot dialog menu required selection of the desired ratio of image to plot, an exercise that sometimes taxed the mathematical agility of the operator. For example, if the paper space drawing was 30 x 42 inches and was to be plotted full size, the plot ratio was 1:1. If it was to be plotted half size, the ratio was 1:2, both easy-to-visualize calculations. If, however, a drawing in paper space was scaled ¾" = 1'-0" and it was desired to plot it at 1" = 1'-0", the ratio was 1.33. Or if a 1/16" scale drawing was to be plotted at 1" = 20', the scales were first converted to ratios. Usually a calculator was needed to do the math, being careful to assign the correct numerator and denominator.

CAD had other characteristics different from hand drafting, as described in other chapters. But computer aided design introduced several new dimensions to the meaning of scale.

Chapter Five: CAD

Black infinity.
Words and digits entering.
Images emerge.

Directing a computer to draw began experimentally in the early 70s. The tools were FORTRAN programming language for the program and the data, key punch cards, a main frame computer, and a Calcomp roller plotter. The task was to program the plotter to draw a perspective of a simple "L"-shaped object. Each of the ordinate intersections was calculated, then programmed, then punched into the cards.

The plotter, state of the art but primitive by today's standards, laboriously drew the outline of the shape in perspective, hidden lines and all. Horizontal lines were drawn with a pen stylus travelling parallel to the roller. Vertical lines were drawn with the same stylus while the roller rotated on its axis. Diagonal lines by a combination of moves. An Etch-a-Sketch toy gave a good illustration of the process.

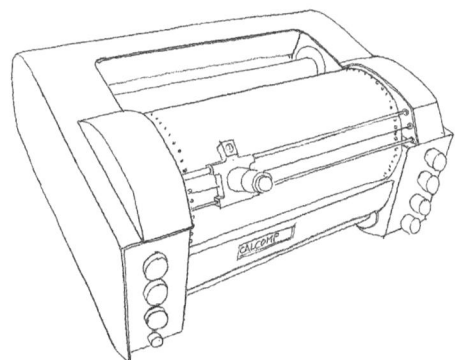

Calcomp Plotter, ca. 1966

Development of the technology progressed quietly. By the early 80s computer aided design and drafting setups became commercially available, though not affordable by most architectural firms. The first applications were for both computer aided design and drafting (CADD), but as the distinction between design and drafting became blurred the term was simplified to CAD.

There were two basic setups: one used a mainframe computer with "dumb" workstations, the other "smart" independent workstations, each with their own computers.

One of the mainframe packages used Digital Equipment Company (DEC) computers. The major mainframe producer of both hardware and software was a company called Intergraph with a product of the same name. Its computers were housed in several refrigerator-sized cabinets and the five or so workstations they could support featured two monitors each. A typical setup cost over $1 million. Large public utilities could afford the investment. Southern Bell installed theirs on raised access floor and used them to record the location of many miles of telephone cable in their territory. A few large and mid sized architectural firms took the plunge.

The independent workstation versions had several companies in competition, each with their proprietary software, hardware, and furniture. The workstations could be connected for mutual support. A setup comparable to the mainframe version cost about the same, so the choice concerned issues such as: what if the mainframe crashed, why invest in several identical programs if one would do the job, and who will still be around next year for support?

In this brief era of the technology the mainframes won, primarily due to the heavy investment of the leading producer, Intergraph.

Personal computers (PCs) changed the whole picture, focusing on the development of competitive CAD software programs based on Microsoft DOS. By the late 80s there were several programs on the market. MicroStation brand, a descendent of Intergraph, offered programs for the PC CAD market, while Intergraph itself continued with software primarily for large process-engineering applications. A CAD program called Versacad was more user-friendly than most, but lived a short life.

The CAD market was soon dominated by AutoCAD from Autodesk Corp., either because of its better software or more aggressive marketing, or both. AutoCAD remained the dominant program, although many offices were invested in MicroStation and swore by it. The two programs found ways to talk to each other and they remained the only competitors in the US.

An office's first use of CAD for a project was an investment with an unknown return. Architectural firms' principals reluctantly acknowledged that payoff would come, but not for a long time in the future. At the same time, offices installed computers to handle word processing and business office applications, installations that brought stressful changes that affected both management and staff. Management researched and selected among competing software and hardware systems, some "bundled" with software as well as hardware, some not.

IBM PC, ca. 1985

Selecting which was best initially or which would remain around for support was a speculative risk. In many cases, the software offered procedures that firms had never even used but that the salesperson assured were indispensable. Then one day there would appear a large tractor-feed printer in the office, spewing out noise and dust and endless stacks of paper.

For staff, including those in the business office, computers required an entire change of culture. Some adapted readily. Some found it was a good time to retire.

The first CAD applications in a firm were often pushed by one or two architects who could see the future, had the boldness to experiment, and received a degree of support from management. Computers, compared to today's equipment, were extremely slow, screens were small, and program commands were limited. Storage space was small and backups were copied onto floppy discs.

CAD was first applied to drawing floor plans for large buildings (why start small?). A large floor plan drawn in what is now known as model space was broken into sheet-size portions, using match lines, much as was required with hand drawn plans. Paper space, which allowed the entire plan to be drawn in model space and subdivided in paper space, was not available until 1990.

CAD provided the ability to easily zoom into and out of the drawing with the control of a few keys or the mouse. Designers could "back up" and view the entire drawing like they had on paper, though the screen was a lot smaller. CAD's black screen and multi-colored lines didn't look like a normal drawing, so many architects could only evaluate the progress of an emerging design if it was plotted. Like with word processing, quality review was easier with a paper copy.

Unfortunately, as tedious as the first computers were at drawing, the plotting process was terrible. And expensive. Plotting was slow and costly enough that check plots would be made perhaps only once every several days. Frustration would boil when the first $100 plot revealed dumb errors that were difficult to visualize on the screen.

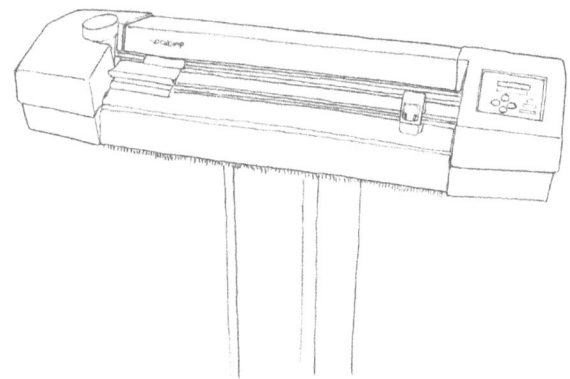

Calcomp Plotter, ca. 1980

At first in some offices only floor plans were drawn on CAD, and then only to a level of partial completion. The CAD drawing indicated the walls, doors and door numbers, room names and numbers, column grids, and toilet fixtures, plus borders and title blocks. From this stage they were plotted on Mylar and completed by hand drafting.

The electronic file was sent to the engineers who continued with their choice of either CAD or paper. Architectural changes made to the basic walls after a certain point were made by hand on the Mylar plot by eradicating the lines and drawing over with pencil. The engineers did the same. The architect drew all the other drawings (elevations, details, schedules, etc) by hand.

The advantages of this method, besides attempting to utilize CAD for its best features, were that the walls were accurately drawn and one workstation could support several projects. That was not a lot, for the skeptics. But CAD survived, mainly because of its promise to get better. There was a pony in there somewhere.

It took several years to expand CAD applications from just floor plans to the entire project. The length of time was partly due to the fact that CAD was well suited for plan drafting, and partly because experienced hand drafters were still available to draw the sections and details.

Drafters, whether trained for hand or for CAD work, were not coming through the pipeline to replace the experienced ones. There were no effective training or apprentice programs for new technical architectural staff. As the experienced drafters matriculated into retirement an office was left with very few who had the training or the demeanor to draw quality details.

Almost all of the young staff entering the office were graduates of schools of architecture. They had not been taught traditional drafting by either hand or CAD. In their first office experience they were put on a computer to draw floor plans and door schedules. They became adept at the computer, but had few mentors to teach them how to draw quality details.

CAD drafting was at first considered a drafting skill, supplemental to normal architectural and engineering services. Accordingly, offices accounted for the time as a separate billing category, charging the time at a "CAD drafting" rate. The practice was based on the concern that CAD drafters would become specialists, higher priced but much more productive than hand drafters. The theory (or hope) was it would be viewed by clients as an added value to standard services so they would willingly pay more.

The conversion totally to CAD was related to lower prices for PC hardware, the improvement of CAD software, and the development of better plotters and printers. The transition from all hand drafting to all CAD took place in the decade of the 90s, and by the turn of the century hand drafting was obsolete.

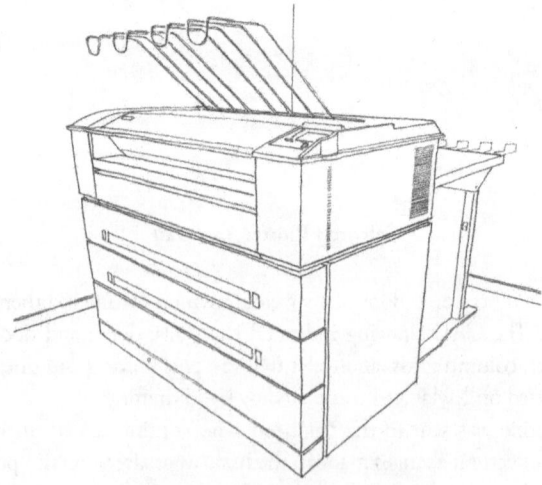

Oce TDS 600 Plotter, ca. 2010

Chapter Five: CAD

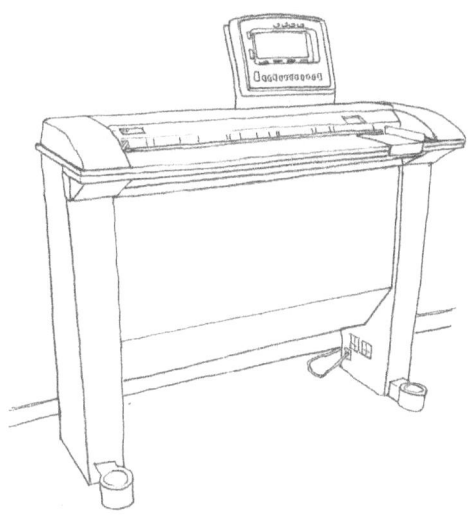

Oce TDS 600 Scanner, ca. 2010

CAD was a cultural as well as a technological revolution, not without human stress. In the drafting room, many of the "old timers" could and did make the change to CAD; many could not or refused to try.

CAD drafting was no longer considered a specialty skill and offices no longer felt the need to either pay or collect different rates for the time.

Soon every architectural work station was equipped with a PC programmed for CAD. They were also programmed for word processing. Architects typed their own letters and memos, and the clerical department was no longer needed.

The amount of work produced per person was definitely greater than it was when all projects were drawn by hand. Seen another way, projects that once required 6 to 8 hand drafters and architects could now be completed by 3 or 4 or even fewer.

Architectural CAD operators usually learned on the job. Architectural schools offered a smattering of CAD courses, but any extensive learning of CAD skills in college probably came from individual effort. Community and technical colleges offered programs of computer-aided design and drafting that were excellent entries to engineering or manufacturing venues.

Architects found the most effective way to learn CAD was in a work environment with a team of experienced associates nearby to answer questions and offer suggestions. Understanding and skill developed rapidly. An interested learner found that experimentation lead to discoveries. Lessons were remembered if learned through frustration. Help was available from the pull-down menu or the 2-inch thick user's guide, but it was more effective to ask your neighbor who probably had the same problem.

That is, as long as your neighbor's computer and the network were kept in good working order.

My operating system's broke, I just want to yell:
Hey computer person come and defrag my Dell!
It's got the blues…Fragmentation blues.

Essential to the productivity of a computerized office was the information technology (IT) guy—the "computer person" of the Fragmentation Blues ditty. Whether embedded in the employee chart or on call from elsewhere, he (historically male but increasingly female) was the person that fixed and repaired hardware and software, maintained the network and the servers, and ordered and installed new equipment. The skills were sometimes learned from college level IT programs, but often only from interest that began in elementary or middle school and was honed through practical experience. It was a skill that didn't even exist before computers.

Usually expert more in the operating system side of a computer than the program application side, the IT person was often not versed in CAD programs. For those difficulties, some of the CAD operators were called on to solve most problems, know when to upgrade, and establish office CAD standards.

Architects currently practicing, if they learned to use hand tools and techniques at all for drawing, no longer do. The tools were all replaced by computers which, for the most part, produced higher quality drawings better and faster.

Computers replaced almost every task in an architect's office which, of course, was either a benefit or a liability. Looking at a monitor all day long, an architect could become isolated from others. Some of the interaction and casual commenting that occurred when large drawings on the board were open to view, was lost. The benefits of being able to easily draw and copy details and specifications was quickly eroded by the liabilities involved when the source was flawed.

Computers became the center of practice. Formerly the first action when arriving at work in the morning was to turn on the desk light, remove the dust cover, and hope the phone didn't ring until some productive work was done; it became turn on the computer and check email. A desk or workstation with a wire-connected PC became the "place" for work.

There is no question that CAD and its current expansion into 3-D modeling and building information management (BIM) is here to stay. For its benefits of speed, clarity, and efficiency, CAD is definitely superior to hand drafting. But perhaps because of its capabilities, CAD can easily allow the user to lose touch with the meaning and purpose of an architectural drawing, which is simply to convey a two dimensional representation from which a three dimensional object can be built.

Electronic media, for the near future at least, must still be converted to a 2-dimensional paper document for distribution to other members of the construction industry.

Following Verse by Richard T. Reep:

Fragmentation Blues

I lie awake at midnight.
Fall asleep at the alarm.
Gridlock on the way to work.
Now half the morning's gone.
This time I shouldn't lose.
Gives me the fragmentation blues.

My password has expired.
My mailbox overflowed
Into my HP printer settings.
Now my downloads won't upload.
But that's old news.
I've got those fragmentation blues.

My operating system's broke
I just want to yell:
Hey computer person come and defrag my Dell!
It's got the blues.
Fragmentation blues.
And when you've done my PC
You can defrag me.

My dollar fifty stapler broke.
My chair just fell apart.
Before I finish one thing,
There are three more jobs to start.
Wish I could take a cruise
And lose those fragmentation blues.

Just as I settle down to work
The phone rings off the hook.
The boss says "Hurry up down there
Our client's here to look."
He's got a real short fuse.
I've got the fragmentation blues.

My operating system's broke
I just want to yell:
Hey computer person come and defrag my Dell!
It's got the blues.
Fragmentation blues.
And when you've done my PC
You can defrag me, as well.

Chapter Six: Documents

Silent language.
One mind speaks to another.
Communicating.

The construction industry was composed of individuals, committees, businesses, corporations—organized groups. The products of an architect's designs became documents for their use. Plans and specs, in the vernacular. Deliverables, in contract language. Some were meant to communicate ideas and gain consensus, some formed the basis of legal contracts, some were for the final record.

Documents, like all aspects of architectural practice, evolved into new types and uses. Generally, they were first prepared on paper.

Cool, white, inviting.
So eager for its first mark.
Intimidating.

Nothing turned on architectural juices more than a fresh new sheet of drawing paper. At the same time, unless mentally prepared to draw, a blank sheet of paper could be daunting. Where to begin. Lou Kahn said he would want to "rub some soil on it" just to make it less challenging for his first line. Asian "sumi-e" (ink wash) painters would meditate for long moments in preparation for applying the first brushstrokes.

Paper, specifically tracing paper, was the preferred drawing media base for architects and engineers (AEs). The term tracing described a transparent or translucent paper. It was used for two purposes.

One was to actually trace images from an underlay. Designers, in developing their ideas, sketched on overlay after overlay, each iteration modifying the previous. They used inexpensive tracing paper, usually more translucent than transparent, which allowed the new image to dominate.

The other purpose for tracing paper was to benefit the reproduction process, a technology based on light passing through an original drawing onto a treated paper sheet that was then chemically developed. In this process the more transparent the original, the better.

One hundred years ago the primary medium for drafting was treated linen. Linen was selected for its ability to accept India ink and for its transparency, since the ink work was traced from a pencil underlay.

After World War II when pencil drafting was common, the primary medium for drafting was vellum, a treated cotton rag paper. The standard product for most offices was Clearprint 1000H vellum. First introduced in 1933, 1000H was paper made from cotton rags treated with chemicals to improve transparency, durability, and longevity. It "took" pencil fairly well – that is to say it was strong enough that adequate pressure could be applied to produce a crisp, dark line with clean edges. When fresh, the line could be completely erased. A line several months old was more difficult to completely erase, but that was a benefit to longevity.

Other available products included a vellum manufactured by K+E (Keuffel and Esser) with a surface texture that, compared to 1000H, allowed the lead to flow more smoothly. It was not as "oily" and the lines could be drawn more dense and crisp. However, it was not as transparent as 1000H and was not commonly used.

K+E Swan Bond was a rag-based paper with little or no treatment. Its surface texture accepted lead very smoothly; hard enough to allow the pencil point to glide, yet with enough tooth to draw out the graphite. It was not transparent enough for tracing, but its clean, white color made it an excellent paper for soft pencil sketching and rendering.

Designers used sketch paper, also called sketch tissue, trash, bumwad, or a number of other localized names, colored either grayish white or yellow. Semi-transparent and inexpensive, it was used for sketching and preliminary drafting work. Sometimes the sketch became the final drawing, so durability was a factor. Some design professionals preferred white, some yellow, some used both. The yellow version, called canary or cedar paper, had a harder surface texture, yielding a better quality pencil line, like K+E Swan Bond.

Treated linen, although originally produced for ink drafting, also accepted lead very well. One side was smooth, the other more fabric-textured. Some federal projects still required linen into the late 50s, but its use after that was rare. Actually it was rare for a client to specify the materials used by the architect; the requirement for linen was for reasons of bureaucratic permanence.

Drafting paper, the manila-colored stiff paper, was used by students in the 50s to learn to letter, draft, or draw freehand sketches. It provided a good tooth for an F lead, but a hard lead required pressure that created a groove that remained after a line was erased.

Illustration board was the preferred media base for student projects in architectural schools in the 50s. Drawings were presented with ink on board. Strathmore and Crescent were standard choices. The medium was a holdover from schools of architecture of the Beaux Arts tradition of a century before. In the 50s there was, thankfully, less emphasis on watercolor washes.

Although a well-drawn presentation on board signified high quality design, according to the standards at the time, the process was very cumbersome for student work. It inhibited creativity. Decision-making was postponed until the last minute. Pencil showed fairly well on board, so the inkwork was reserved for heavier profile lines and poché (infill) of the wall thickness in floor plans and sections.

Students spent a great deal of time learning to use ruling pens, keeping them clean and sharp, and cleaning up spills and blotches. Current architecture students have much more freedom of choice of media.

Polyester Mylar began to replace 1000H in the 70s for drafting in AE offices. It was more durable and transparent than vellum and could withstand the rough use it usually received, especially at the edges of the sheet.

Plastic lead was used on Mylar for its ability to produce lines with some of the clarity of ink and the workability of graphite. Graphite "took" very well on Mylar, but plastic was preferred because it would smear less. Flexible and bendable, plastic lead required a fair amount of experience and patience in order to draw consistent quality linework while avoiding constant lead breakage. With a hard lead the lines would be weak, and too much pressure would flex or break the lead. Too soft and the lines would be fuzzy.

Mylar's other characteristic was its dimensional stability, allowing it to be an excellent medium for overlay drafting with pin bar registration, a process that had a short life span in the 80s. Precisely located pre-punched holes in the top edge of the sheet allowed multiple layers to be overlaid onto the pin bar and be accurately aligned with each other. Mylar's transparency allowed several sheets to be stacked, each with a different layer of information added to supplement the base layer.

The base sheet included the walls, doors, and other graphic elements. Other information needed for a complete plan drawing was drawn on overlays registered on the pin bar. Printing of the appropriate combination of sheets was done on a flat bed printer, pinned together so as to maintain alignment.

The pin bar process required a fair amount of pre-planning and drawing control management, a discipline not prevalent in every architect's office. The process disappeared after CAD was accepted and provided xrefs (cross references), an electronic version of base sheets with overlays.

Reproduction

Architects in the 21st century were still known for producing blueprints even though blueprints diminished in use in the 1940s and had not been used at all after the 70s. The blueprint process, developed in France in the 1860s, used a chemically treated paper to reproduce an image from a transparent medium. In the early days, the light used for exposure was daylight. K+E offered a printing device whose frame slid out through an open window. The result, as the name suggests, showed white lines on a blue background.

Blueprinting was largely replaced by diazo blueline printing in the 1940s. Some offices even into the 70s, however, still preferred blueprints for record documents, since the paper was heavier and the image more permanently stable.

The diazo process was originally called whiteprinting to distinguish it from the process it was intended to replace. Developed by the Netherlands company Océ in the 1920s, it became the standard method of reproduction for the design profession and remained so until replaced by plotters. In the diazo process, the lines on a transparent original, the tracing, were transferred by ultraviolet light to a chemically treated paper which was then developed with ammonium hydroxide fumes. Depending on the type of print paper, the process would produce blueline, blackline, or brown line (Van Dyke) prints on a relatively white background.

Many medium and large firms in the 70s installed a print machine in the office, provided they could ventilate the ammonia fumes. The machines were simple to operate, so were used for everyday check prints. Print shops (called reprographic companies, or repro houses) offered competitive services for large volume production printing, with convenient pickup and delivery.

Sepia prints were produced by the diazo printing process. The name referred to the color of the printed image. Sepias were produced with special semi transparent paper or Mylar. They served as copies of original drawings, themselves capable of being revised and printed by diazo reproduction.

To make a drawing revision on a sepia print, the printed lines were removed with two-component liquid eradicator. It came in small bottles with an applicator brush attached to the lid, like nail polish bottles. The first component eradicated the image, the second "stopped" the chemical process. A good quality sepia print allowed a good quality revision, but a print too dense, with a lot of background, became blotchy, since some of the surrounding background was also eradicated. This medium was not missed.

No reproduction machine revolutionized office work more than the plain paper copy machine using Xerographic technology. AE offices benefitted as much from this technology as others for letter-sized paper, given its ability to make copies of opaque as well as transparent originals. Gone were the days when to get a copy of a document the original was sent to a repro house for a poor quality "Photostat" copy to be delivered the next day.

Expansion of plain paper copying technology to drawing-sized sheets in the 90s completed the evolution of reproduction for architects. Diazo printing became obsolete. Scanning technology allowed the original itself to be bond, like office copiers, and the reproduction to be either a paper copy or an electronic file. Similarly, an electronic image, rather than a paper copy, could be "fed in" to the scanner or plotter.

Sheet Sizes

Drawing sheet sizes in America became standardized to units of 22, 24, 30, 34, 36, 42, and sometimes 48 inches. Architectural drawings were usually 30 x 42 inches. Engineers preferred 24 x 36 inch sheets, but for projects in which they were in a consulting role they used the sheet size dictated by the architect. Civil engineers, even those on the team, drew on 24 x 36 because civil engineering review agencies insisted on that size. These standard sizes bridged the shift from hand to electronic drafting.

When plotters and scanners became available, full size reproduction of 30 x 42 inch sheets was reserved for reviewing agencies, bidding, and the construction field office. Copies for office and review use were usually printed at half-size (15 x 21 inches) or 11 x 17, which was not "to scale", but very convenient.

Military agencies preferred 22 x 34 inch drawings, primarily because a half-size copy was printable to scale on 11 x 17 inch paper. That size was easier to handle and store than larger sheets. The agencies also standardized the size of lettering so it was readable at half size.

Titles and Borders

Until the 1960s projects were drawn on sheets cut at the drawing board from bulk rolls of vellum. A bulk roll of vellum was expensive and not to be wasted. An office provided rolls of either the project standard sheet size width (such as 30 inches) or length; the paper was cut at the drafter's desk using a mat knife or by ripping it up against a triangular scale tucked under the roll. With another technique, called the "Chicago cut", the drafter unrolled the paper to the required length, turned it and the roll over, back rolled it to press a crease at the proper dimension, then sheared the paper at the crease with a flat scale.

Margins and borders were drawn by hand with pencil. The outer margin, called the trim line, was approximately ¼ or ½ inch from the edge, designating the size of the print image and providing a sacrificial margin for cuts and tears. The image border was approximately ½ inch inside of the trim on the right, top and bottom, and 1 inch or so on the left edge for binding.

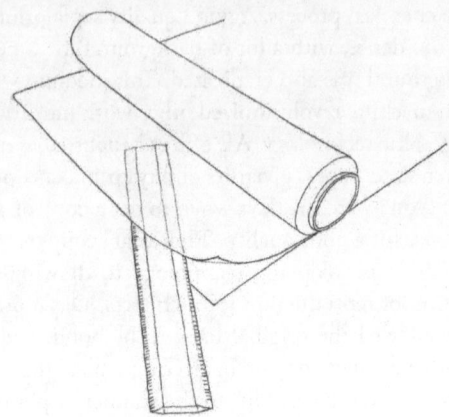

The Chicago Cut—cutting a drawing-sized sheet from a roll

For small projects the title block was drawn by hand. For large projects a rubber stamp was made. Stamped title blocks tended to produce inconsistent images. Quality depended on the care provided by the stamper and the condition of the stamp pad. The image could be weak on one edge, smeared, or out of alignment.

In the 80s, peel-and-stick transparent media printed on office copiers allowed title blocks to be pre-printed and applied even for small projects. For large projects, offices purchased precut sheets with pre-printed title blocks and borders.

The title block was traditionally located in the lower right corner. In the 60s and 70s, firms began to move it to occupy the entire the right-hand edge. The lettering oriented either to the bottom or to the right or both. As with stand-up vs. sit-down drafting tables, this new location became a controversy between the old-timers and the new designers.

The title block in the lower right corner provided a more economical use of drawing space, being only as large as needed for the project. It was a modest summary of the required information. But this location left a rectangular drawing space with a notch out of a corner—a graphic flaw for designers educated in the Modern polemic.

A title block along the entire edge, although requiring more space, left a pure rectangular area for the drawing. It also allowed a larger presentation of the firm's name and, becoming more common, a bold logo. When a set of prints was rolled up, always print-side out, the logo was on display.

The tradition behind the lower right corner for the title block may have been derived from the tradition of artists to sign that corner of their painting as a statement of authorship. The architect's or the firm's name in that corner continued the tradition.

A title block in the lower right of a sheet defined the difference between a drawing and a text document. The sequence of information in a drawing was just the opposite of that on a text document or business letter. On a business letter, the information on the top left began with the author or the firm name, the date, the recipient, the subject, and then the body of text. A drawing was just the reverse. The drawing itself started at the upper and left portion of the sheet; the title information was on the right or the bottom right.

The distinction was of interest to the person who cataloged and filed the document. An image on 8½ x 11 inch paper was a text document if the title information was on the top left, and a drawing if the title information was on the bottom right. It belonged in either the administrative files or the drafting room project files.

Mounting Drawings

Paper drawings were taped or thumb-tacked to a wall for informal presentations (pin-ups). For important groups, like clients, prints of the drawings were mounted on boards. Illustration board was used until foam-core board was available.

In the 50s the drawing was adhered to the board with rubber cement. Sounds simple, but it was not. The process was tedious and stressful. This is how it went:

1. Delay design decisions so the reproduction was made at the last minute, leaving minimum time for mounting and no time for do-over.

2. Lay the board on the floor over a waste paper underlay. Pour rubber cement from a one gallon can onto the board. Spread it evenly with a flat-edged tool like a drawing triangle. Spread the excess onto the waste paper.

3. Lay the drawing face down on the floor over another paper underlay. Apply rubber cement to the back of the drawing, same as the back of the board. Spread the excess onto the waste paper.

4. Let the rubber cement dry for a few minutes. Scrape up any puddles that dried too slow.

5. Two (minimum) people pick up the drawing by the corners and turn it over. Be careful to not have a rubber-cemented surface contact another (it will not release).

6. Carry the drawing over the board. Lower the drawing toward the board, keeping the drawing taut. One handler slowly lowers one end to the board, carefully aligning it with the corners of the board. The other keeps the other end off the board, not letting the drawing sag in the middle. Do not let go of the corners!

7. When aligned, let the drawing adhere to the board at the right-hand corner, then the left. Slowly allow the drawing to make contact from there to the other side, while keeping it taut. During this action a third person, using a clean triangle, strokes the drawing, flattening bubbles, preventing wrinkles. Poke stubborn bubbles with a No 11 blade to let out the air.

8. When complete, trim the drawing. If it is crooked, trim the board.

9. Remove the excess rubber cement by rolling into a ball with the fingers and flick it at your partner as he rushes to the meeting.

Spray-mount adhesive relieved some of this mess, but it was still cumbersome. It was supposed to be sprayed outdoors to not poison your associates. Reprographic companies offered mounting services that, although expensive, were a great deal less stressful and were better quality. Some even performed at the last minute.

Text

Design professionals produced, in addition to drawings, specifications and a great deal of other material in text form such as correspondence, programs, reports, meeting minutes, and the like. The tools, machines, and technology for this work evolved, as it did for offices in other businesses. The basic text-producing device was the manual typewriter.

Manual typewriters were replaced in the 1950s by electric typewriters. The IBM Selectric became the office standard for almost 30 years. Though a superb machine, it still typed through a carbon ribbon onto a piece of paper. Errors were carefully corrected one by one.

A development late in the typewriter era was a machine that provided a delay between the key touch and its action onto the ribbon; a delay that theoretically allowed the typist to realize and correct a typo before the imprint was made.

Word processors arrived in the 1980s. The first versions were stand-alone devices that used large floppy discs for storage and proprietary printers. They were permanently replaced by PCs with improved word-processing software. As much as Microsoft was vilified for its aggressive marketing strategies, it provided the benefit of standardization of programs for word processing and spread sheets, allowing diverse businesses to easily communicate.

IBM Selectric Typewriter

Word processing also changed a major part of a firm's staff structure. Project team members began using a PC to originate and type their own letters and other text documents. Before PCs, a project manager wrote a memo in longhand, sent it to a typist for a draft, reviewed the draft, then waited for the final corrected copy to return for signature. Since not many architects were proficient at using a typewriter, it was thought not possible that a document could be effectively composed and typed in the same operation. Word processing changed all that. The clerical staff was no longer needed.

Reproduction of text also followed the progress of other businesses. Systems evolved from carbon paper to stencil (mimeograph) technology using waxed paper, to spirit duplicators, to photostats (photographic process) and thermal printers (Thermofax). All had their advantages and drawbacks. The drawbacks basically served to make reproduction of text documents costly and time consuming and therefore done no more than required. Plain paper scanners and printers were much easier to use. And to overuse.

Future Documents

The basic documents in architectural practice, the "deliverables", will be drawings and specs. Even though originating in computers, they will be printed on paper. Printed images and words remain so ubiquitous it is difficult to imagine the construction industry getting along without them.

On the other hand, CAD/CAM (computer aided design and manufacturing) has become common to most manufacturing industries, so it is reasonable to expect and foresee it will be applied to the construction industry as well.

Imagine a completely paperless practice. A structural engineer's 3-D CAD drawings of a steel structure will convey a 3-dimensional view to the architect for coordinating on screen, to the general contractor for pricing and scheduling, and to the steel fabricator for direct CAD/CAM input to the cutting and welding shop. There will be no need for printing, no need for shop drawings. Mechanical and Electrical engineering designs will be similar.

Other parts of the building design will be conveyed electronically rather than printed. Millwork shops, many of which currently fabricate cabinet panels with CAD/CAM devices that eliminate the need for hand-operated measuring tapes, table saws, and routers, will input the architect's cabinet design directly into their computers. Door and hardware schedules will be electronically conveyed to the suppliers.

Architectural elements are another matter. Since bulldozers and backhoes will be operated by humans for quite a while longer, the sitework drawings will be printed for the equipment operators. Roof and flashing details are an assemblage of many parts in several sequences and installed by humans. They will continue to be printed, as well.

The caveat for a paperless construction industry lies in the risk of eliminating checks and balances. Manufacturers, who make multiple copies, use models and prototypes to develop designs before committing to the production process. AEs and contractors, who produce custom-designed buildings, have only one chance to get it right. If the building cost must be predicted and committed in the beginning, the pricing documents must describe the design in as much detail as possible.

Since the design will be built only once, the design and construction team will be assembled for just that one project. Team members will bring their own practices and methods to the process. Printing the drawings and specs on paper so everyone can review, coordinate, and comment may continue to be a large part of future practice.

Chapter Seven: Images

Dry lifeless image.
Feel the sun touch the façade.
Reawakening.

When asked to talk to an audience an architect presented a slide show. More images than talk. The slides were of the architect's favorite projects, more than likely his or her own. If several boxes came, the audience was in for a long evening.

Color renderings, large format photos, models, and brochures were basic to an architect's image portfolio as well. For the creative process, study models were as easy as sketches, and detailed models were the most effective for representing the design. Each medium had its own purposes. The one chosen was intended to bring to life the qualities of the design concept.

Slides

Of all the image media produced by architects, color slides were the favorite. They were inexpensive, portable, and versatile. A good slide image could be produced by in-house staff. A professional photographer could produce an excellent one.

Slide was a term that originally referred to a photo transparency mounted in glass that was "slid" into position between a light and a lens in a lantern device, later called a projector. The medium standardized in the 1940s to 35 millimeter (mm) wide color positive film developed and set into 2 x 2 inch cardboard mounts.

Color photography based on 35 mm cameras and color slide film ruled the architectural photo scene until the digital age. While large format cameras and film were required for high quality photos for publication, 35 mm was preferred for projected images. Cameras of the rangefinder design based on 35 mm film originally appeared in the 30s and were widely used for hand-held work. Single lens reflex (SLR) gear developed in the late 50s became the new standard.

Kodak Kodachrome film was preferred by amateurs and professionals alike until its "retirement" from the market in the 2009. It was considered having the best quality for color rendition, sharpness, and longevity. It was developed and mounted only by specialized labs. Until 1954 the purchase price of a roll of Kodachrome included a mailer pouch, used to send the exposed film to a Kodak lab for developing, mounting, and returning (in several days or even weeks).

Kodak with their Ektachrome, Agfa, Fuji and others produced color positive film that could be developed into slides overnight in more readily available labs. Although the color was considered of lesser quality and longevity than Kodachrome, the films were faster for low light conditions and less expensive.

Kodachrome slides could be printed, but at some expense and time. For everyday work (snapshots), color negative film like Kodak Kodacolor or Fuji Fujicolor was used. The film was developed in neighborhood outlets at reasonable prices. It was preferred for reference work, surveys of existing buildings, and informal records.

CHAPTER SEVEN: IMAGES 49

Kodachrome slide

Ektachrome Slide

Projectors

Several versions of projectors were designed in the 40s and 50s. In some the slides were fed one by one. In others from trays shaped like rectangles (like the Kodak Cavalcade), towers, ferris-wheels or merry-go-rounds (like the Kodak Carousel). The Carousel, introduced in 1961, rose to dominate the field for almost 40 years.

After accepting the invitation to present, the architect's first question was "will you be providing the projector?" Both parties, until the late 90s, knew they were talking about a Kodak Carousel. The speaker brought only the trays.

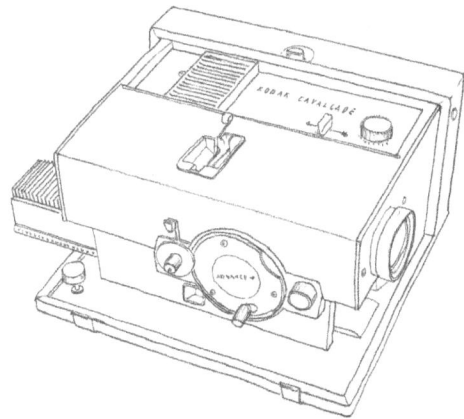
Kodak Cavalcade Projector, ca. 1955

The equipment for the architect's slide show would be provided from the office's supply of several Carousels and portable screens, all in various stages of repair, and trays and trays of slides. If the same or similar talk was to be repeated the slides were stored in the trays, which were housed in cardboard boxes approximately 10 x 10 x 2½ inches. The office's permanent collection was kept in loose leaf binders with vinyl pages with pockets for the slides. Over the years, thousands of slides accumulated, requiring the time and effort of a dedicated "librarian" to maintain the value of the information.

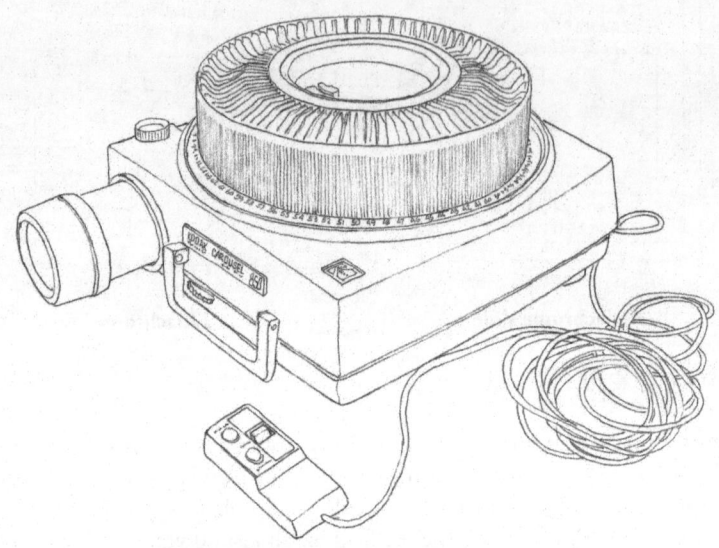

Kodak Carousel Projector, ca. 1990

After slides were replaced by digital images, offices still had their old slide library stored somewhere and wondered what to do with it. If they went through the expense of digitizing the slides they would have a record as easy to store and sort as their file of digital photos. That was a big if, overcast with consideration of the quality of scanning technology, doubts about the future of digital records, and realization of the costs. The old slides probably remained in boxes, to be dealt with another day.

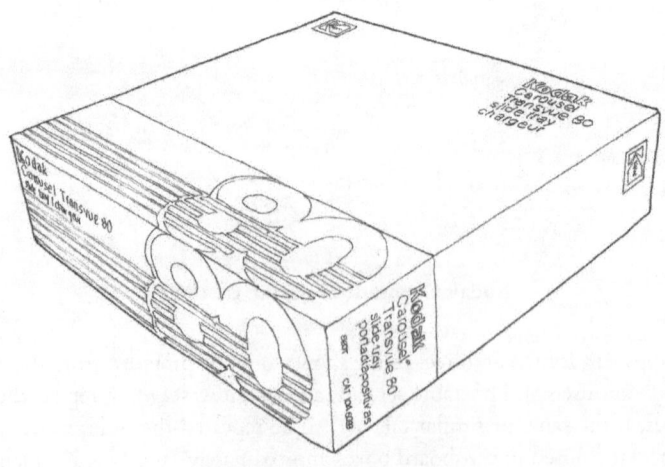

Carousel Slide Tray Storage Box

In the 90s, Microsoft PowerPoint computer images projected by video projectors made photo slides and projectors obsolete. PowerPoint images were also called slides even though they didn't "slide" into place like the cardboard versions. It was a convenient carry-over term.

Video projection technology struggled at first. Early portable projectors cost in the range of $6,000, image quality was poor, and repairs were expensive. Gradually, prices fell and quality improved. Good quality video projectors became affordable for most architects. They were portable enough that, even if the client promised to supply the equipment, the architect brought it and a laptop to the presentation. The standard travel kit included a backup CD, connection cables, extension power cords, and a screen. Also a tech-knowledgable operator.

Renderings

After slide shows and blueprints, architects were best known for the "architect's rendering". Renderings were often a contract requirement of the project following the design development or construction documents phases. Although most architects could prepare a decent black and white sketch of their idea, not many could, or would, produce a color rendering of publication quality. To avoid taking the time and effort to construct a perspective layout and apply the artwork, they relied on outside renderers.

Commercial renderers were usually available locally. Many groups offered a national or even international practice. Some were artists, not renderers or delineators, as they were sometimes called. The work of Hugh Ferriss and Helmut Jacoby survived to attest to its artistic value.

Rendering media included every type used in the commercial art profession. The larger commercial groups (houses) used production-line processes, with specialists for perspective construction, background, trees, people, cars, window reflections, and other details. The order form was extensive, asking questions like: the desired racial mix of figures, color samples of materials, and appropriate species of trees and plants.

Some clients insisted if a specific tree or bush was illustrated in the rendering, it must then appear at the completed building. In that case the architect had to provide the complete approved landscape design to the renderer.

Computer-produced renderings replaced hand-drawn/painted versions. National rendering firms offered these services, but many architects had at least one computer-savvy person who could handle Photoshop or the more extensive 3-D programs. Moving "fly-through" images could be produced in even a small architectural office that had sufficient computer capacity. 3D rendering programs allowed the rendering to become more of a design development tool. The designer could design while the renderer rendered.

Completed renderings were handled much as art work: mounted and framed. Painted renderings were photographed for the record. Computer generated work was printed and mounted, or presented via power point or live screen projection.

Photos

Architectural photography was a specialty that developed skilled practitioners. Artists like G. E. Kidder Smith, Alexandre Georges, Balthazar Korab, and the Hedrich-Blessing

Group were instrumental in depicting and preserving the images of significant architecture (and sometimes in elevating the value of the not so significant). Architects promoted their work by celebrating their accomplishments, their buildings. Services of a professional architectural photographer were essential.

The images showed good lighting, proper point of view, no keystoning, no clutter, and were devoid of human activity (a subject of derision from critics of modern architecture). Photographer's assistants watered the foreground pavements with a hose to liven the colors. Stray electric wires, if they couldn't be avoided in the lens, could be dashed or cropped out in the printing process. Photographers of residential interiors rearranged the owner's furniture or even brought their own.

Photos were printed for inclusion in the architect's brochure, for display in the office, for submittal to design awards programs, and for publication. Publication in the national architectural press, the magazines, was the goal for many architects. High quality professional photos were required.

Architectural magazines declined both in number and in the amount of feature stories of current design projects after 2000. Similarly, most offices stopped producing printed brochures. Computerized client presentations were projected on a screen with a video projector. As a result, high quality still images from large format cameras were less in demand. Photos taken by competent photographers, whether professional or not, using good quality SLR digital cameras or even point-and-shoot versions, sufficed for most presentation tasks.

Models

A story is told that Eero Saarinen's eureka moment for the concept for the Kresge Auditorium at Yale happened at breakfast one morning as he turned over his half-grapefruit and sliced off 3 sides. Floor plan and section drawings followed. It is not known whether the "model" survived the trip to the office.

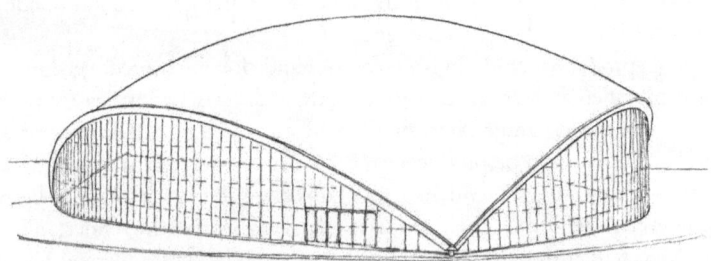

Kresge Auditorium, Yale University, 1955. Eero Saarinen, architect

Study models were an excellent medium for a designer's iterative process. Architectural students learned the value of study models early in their studio work. They found that even a rough study model could help them and their teacher, and later their client, visualize an architectural concept better than drawings.

CHAPTER SEVEN: IMAGES   53

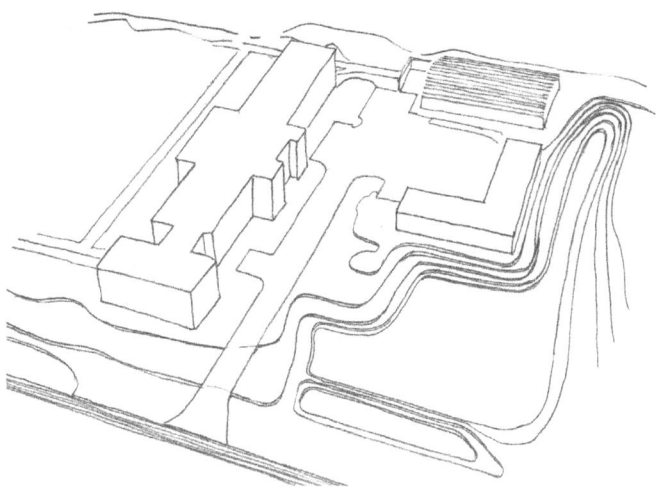

Study Model with Chip Board Contours and Foam Buildings

In the period when architectural pedagogy was founded on the principles of Modern Architecture, students used plexiglass for walls. Cardboard or balsa wood was overlaid to represent the solid material between the floor-to-ceiling glazing. Window mullions were scratched into the plexi with sharp tools.

Practicing architectural designers constructed concept models of chip board, balsa, basswood, and other sheet materials. New York firm Hardy Holzman and Pfeiffer in the 80s gained notoriety by building conceptual site models with colored paper tubes, yarn, product

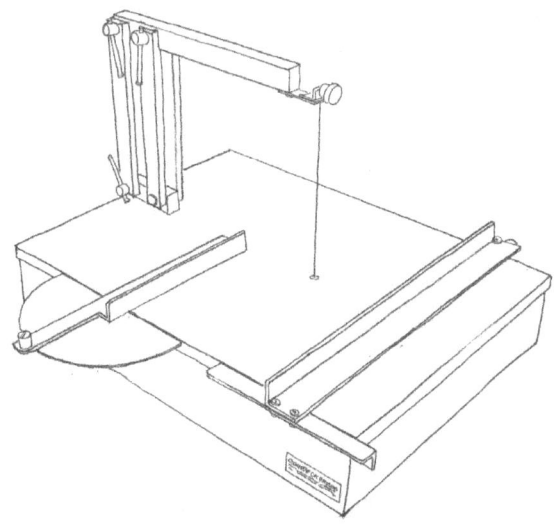

Hot Wire Cutter

boxes, and other found objects. Model building was a critical part of the practice of Frank Gehry, who developed a design first with sketches but quickly moved to paper study models. Louis Kahn, when designing the master plan for downtown Philadelphia in 1961, produced a large model made entirely out of Plasticine modeling clay.

Model building on flat sites was easy. Sloping sites were a challenge. Building a credible model that represented the slopes required much of the time allotted to the entire task. The generally used technique involved cutting a cardboard sheet for each contour—the cardboard thickness represented the desired contour interval—and gluing one sheet on top of another, producing a stepped surface. The thinner the sheet, the more the steps represented the natural ground. But the more material consumed.

Materials chosen for the contours depended on not only their cost and time requirement, but whether the model would be used for presentation. Besides chip board, choices included illustration board (hard to cut), and corrugated cardboard (rough appearance but inexpensive). When hot-wire cutters became available, thin sheets of polystyrene foam were used. The same hot wire cutter was used to shape foam blocks for building masses.

Presentation models of the final design were built by specialists with national or international practices. Before CAD, the models were hand built of basswood or other stable material and either painted or left natural. With CAD, model builders used the electronic drawings from the architect to input directly into a CAD-CAM machine to cut all the parts out of plexiglass. The process and the material allowed representation of details, even handrail pickets, at a small scale. The parts were then assembled by hand and painted. The results were extremely realistic and were often photographed to substitute for a painted rendering. Understandably, these models were expensive, ordered only for significant projects.

In the early 21st century, virtual models prepared by 3D computer programs were used in most offices, replacing physical models. The programs were economical enough to be used even during concept and schematic phases of design.

Brochures

In the 50s architects gained commissions by reputation, word of mouth, and by association with the "network"—passive means, by later standards. In the 60s and 70s, when marketplace competition demanded more active pursuit of commissions, it became imperative to have a brochure describing the firm's work and capabilities.

The development of a quality office brochure could be a stressful undertaking, entailing hours of discussion amongst opinionated design principals to agree on colors, typeface, and graphics of the document, let alone how to portray the design philosophy of the firm. Sometimes the need to develop a new brochure was used as an incentive to hone the firm's mission statement.

Brochures were often prepared and printed by outside professional graphics firms. Accordingly, they were expensive. Due to the high cost, the print order was large. Either the projects or the graphic style became out of date before the supply ran out.

Some offices preferred a loose leaf "modular" format that could be custom organized for specific types of work. Response to a request for proposal (RFP) could quickly be assembled from a library of project data sheets.

In the 80s federal agencies began to require standard formats for proposal responses. The General Services Administration (GSA) developed the 254-255 project information forms for their work. The format was followed by state and local agencies and even large private clients. Printed brochures were no longer required in the submittal nor were they even allowed, and so were no longer produced by most firms. They were replaced by web sites.

Firms considered a good web site an effective and less costly way to promote themselves to potential clients, future employees, and the general public. A high quality web site was more effective than a brochure to portray the firm, as long as it was kept up to date. Most firms contracted outside website designers for both initial design and periodic maintenance.

Interviews

Up until the 90s, an architect preparing for an interview was faced with making a number of choices. None was easy, and there was never enough time to prepare.

Should the images be slides or boards or both? If the goal was to show off earlier work only, a slide show was an easy choice. If it required the use of charts and graphics, boards were better. If the audience was large, however, boards may not be large enough to be seen be all. If both would be effective, both slides and boards were prepared.

The presentation outline was determined by the team leaders. Graphics were drawn and colored by the staff. An office with access to a photo studio transferred the chart information to slides. If boards were prepared, graphics were printed and mounted (see the Documents chapter for mounting experiences). After the 70s it could be sent out to a repro house for printing and mounting. Either way, it was always at the last minute.

Boards required the use of easels, another logistical complication. The office's supply may be scattered, or the broken ones still broken. If the interview was out of town, easels and boards were cumbersome travel companions. Boards were stuffed into portfolios that, along with the easels, may or may not fit into the travel vehicles.

PowerPoint and video projectors arrived in the 90s to save the day. Interviews settled into slide presentations. Eliminating boards was a great relief. Slides, even of charts, schedules, sketches, photos, and combinations of all were easy to prepare. The team leaders had direct involvement in preparing both the information and the graphic composition. Last minute changes were easy to make.

Further, a laptop computer could display a CAD image on both its monitor and, through a projector, a screen, allowing live interaction between the presenters and the audience. CAD was not only a design tool, it was a presentation medium.

By 2010, electronic media offered alternatives to or total replacements for all of the manual image-making processes.

Chapter Eight: Firms

One is not enough.
One plus one equals many.
Many becomes one.

In the late 1800s, the beginning of an urban building boom, a typical architectural firm had a very simple organization. Design was provided by the principal in the form of sketches; drafting was performed in the drafting department by technical staff and apprentices managed and trained by a chief draftsman. The principals may have been the only members with a professional architectural education. A license was not required; Illinois, in 1897, being the first state to establish the requirement.

The path to becoming an architect, and a future principal, began with employment at such a firm as an apprentice with or without the architectural education. Frank Lloyd Wright began his career at the age of 20 in the office of Joseph Silsbee in Chicago. Clarence Johnston and Cass Gilbert both apprenticed at the St. Paul firm of Abraham Radcliffe while in high school. Bruce Goff, an architect in Oklahoma, began this track in 1916 at the age of 12.

At that time a relatively limited amount of information was required in order to direct the construction of a building. Architectural drawings for small projects included, in addition to common architectural views, the basic elements of the heating and plumbing systems, lighting, and convenience outlets. For example, the number of cells for the hot water radiator in each exterior room was indicated on the architectural floor plan. Although mechanical systems were designed by engineering firms for larger projects, for smaller ones technical details for such systems were completed by specialty contractors, an early form of design-build.

Foundation design in many projects was the responsibility of the construction contractor. For projects on urban mid-block sites, only the front façade was "designed" by the architect. There was need for only minimal project management both in the office and the construction site. Good quality was expected of and provided by the construction trades.

On the other hand, most of the parts and pieces in the finished building were designed in the office since there were few manufactured catalog items available. Architects or drafters designed items such as radiator and convector covers, elevator cages, restroom marble stalls, window sash and frames, and decorative friezes. Architects exercised their creative skills designing these components. The terra cotta tile work sketched by Louis Sullivan and George Elsmlie on the Carson Pirie Scott building in Chicago, and drafted by the staff, is a prime example.

As technology progressed and work volume increased in the 20th century, offices gradually grew larger. Skills and specialties such as specifications writers, construction administration (CA) specialists, and millwork detailers were added. By the 30s, a large office may have had a marketing or politically-connected principal, a design principal, a technical principal, several project managers (architects each managing several projects), a chief draftsman, drafters both new and experienced, a specs writer, a field man for CA, and clerical staff. Many of the staff, especially the experienced drafters, stayed with the same firm for their entire career.

This organization of an architectural firm—a few architect principals, specialist skills, and many career drafters—remained the standard until into the 70s. Firms were generally organized into departments, based on the phases of the project.

Design was done in three distinct phases: Schematics (SC), Design Development (DD), and Contract Documents (CD). The design concept (which may have been sketched on the proverbial paper napkin) and Schematics were drawn by the design principal with an assistant. Design Development was a distinct phase performed by the staff in the design department. A job captain in the production department drafting room then took over the Construction Documents, or working drawings, with the drafters. There was a clear transition between these phases—one must be complete before the next one started.

The client was required to "sign off" on the design at the completion of each phase. A well disciplined office would not move a project into the production department for CDs until the DDs were complete, and there was a clear definition of what was meant by completion. The designer visited the drafting room during CDs only to clarify the intent or resolve design conflicts; certainly not to change a previously approved design.

A project manager provided in-house administrative continuity through all the phases. Coordination with the engineers was the responsibility of the job captain. The principals assured that quality control was consistent.

The departmental organization of an architectural office evolved. Degreed and registered architects began replacing the traditional drafting staff. Architects, even young interns, had more of an "ownership" relationship with an office and became involved in marketing and project management as well as design. Becoming an increasing proportion of the total staff and by simply asserting more authority, young architects began to change the structure of the firm and the way a project was produced. The very process with which building design teams were educated and organized was affected. The dwindling supply of trained drafters occurred at the same time.

In the 1970s mid- and large-size architectural firms began marketing themselves as team-oriented rather than departmentalized. The pitch was that the project would be designed and managed by an assigned group from beginning to end, rather than being handed off from department to department as each phase progressed. Departments were said to be stodgy and impersonal; the client would benefit from the improved service and design quality gained from a dedicated project team.

This marketing point worked for a while, but it soon became a ho-hum item for selection committees. The organization of an architect's office either didn't mean much to the client, or they understood it well enough to know that all firms were organized that way, or else they were savvy enough to not quite believe it would provide better service.

Most interviews no longer discussed firm organization except perhaps for the requirement to identify the "day-to-day point of contact". The project team method, however, remained.

Quality of service was the responsibility of the team leader. Design oriented firms (those that collected design awards) emphasized that their project would be led by a Project Architect, whereas the team leader in a rival firm was merely a Project Manager. Their point was that "architecture" would be in control; "management" was subservient—the project manager worked for the design architect, not the other way around.

This distinction was presented primarily in the marketing stage, since once underway the nature and schedule of the project determined whether and when management was more critical than design. Although both leaders were registered architects, many architectural designers were not good organizers, and many good managers were mediocre designers.

By the 80s, the profile of a contemporary architectural firm was: several principals (one focused on design, one on marketing, one on technical), associates (one led a market sector, a territory, a studio, etc), project managers (or project architects), support architects (either newly registered or graduate interns), interior designers, and specifications producers. Some offices had a separate group for CA services, otherwise CA services were performed by the project manager or associate. Almost all of these persons were graduate and registered architects. A grouping was called a team or studio, not to be called a department (although the stigma was waning).

The team for the design phases of a typical medium-sized project had a principal or associate, project manager or architect, and several support architects. The support staff quantity and experience varied with the type of project and the phase of design. At certain times specifications producers and other specialists worked on it. Interior designers were assigned from the beginning or only during certain phases.

All of the traditional phases, Schematics, DD, and CD, were produced by the same team. The distinction between the phases was often blurred and sometimes a phase was skipped entirely (DD for example). Governmental or military clients that required design progress submittals in traditional intervals may have provided the only projects requiring such phasing.

Some members of the team followed the project from beginning to end, but only the same number as would have in a departmentalized firm. The difference was that the contemporary firm offered a project team with more professionals who were better able to deal with the demands of a more complicated design and construction environment. The challenge was to train young staff members to maintain quality control in the face of ever-increasing staff turnover trends. Young architects tended to change firms a great deal more often than career drafters did.

A significant difference in a CAD office compared to a pre-CAD office was a much smaller staff was required for the same size project. Another difference was that the team members each performed a greater variety of tasks. One or two project architects performed code research, product research, building condition surveys, schematics, design development and contract documents, coordination with engineers, presentation drawings, shop drawing review, field visits during construction, punch-out inspections, and project close-out. In addition, many also provided initial client and sub-consultant negotiations and agreements. An architect became a generalist with specialist skills.

The floor plan of the architect's office no longer had an identifiable design studio or drafting room since every work station could be performing any task. Even the front office, no longer needing a clerical pool, could be reduced to a reception desk. A firm could be equally at home in an office building loft or a former residence.

When the founding principals retired, the successor principals had a different attitude toward each other and to the organization of the firm than the founders. Whether being "tapped" by the founders or having maneuvered themselves into position, they were probably not as bonded to each other as the founders once were. Each could be expected to have a client base and lead their own marketing and design efforts. Technical skills and quality control, although no less critical, were at risk of receiving less attention in the organization. The structure of the firm became much looser, resembling an association of several small firms joined together.

The associative type of firm, although appearing less organized, was very effective and flexible, able to quickly meet the demands of a changing market. The structure was pioneered by The Architect's Collaborative (TAC), the firm founded in 1945 by Walter Gropius in Boston.

Sizes of architectural firms varied from one person sole proprietors to several hundred. The vast majority, even those fairly large, were classified by the government, according to dollar volume, as small businesses.

The business form for most firms was corporation of some sort (business, professional, Subchapter S, LLC, or other), although the form was not usually a factor in determining their method of practice. A few were partnerships, but the exposure of personal liability inherent in this form made it less attractive.

Titles for the staff, such as partner (even in corporations), principal, associate, president, vice president, varied from firm to firm depending on its size and culture. Usually, however, staff titles referred to function—project architect, associate architect, etc.—rather than position in the corporate hierarchy.

Forces that direct the organization of future firms include these trends:

- Increasing number of outside consultants for such tasks as cost estimating, building code review, accessibility code review, acoustics, security, building commissioning, hazardous materials, vertical transportation, planning, traffic planning, LEED certification, and more.
- Firms that provide design-only services teamed with architect-of-record services from another firm. This grouping is similar to the departmental organization of the past.
- Clients such as the military who require design services only. CA services will be provided by other entities.
- Firms that specialize in certain building types such as justice or health care.
- Firms that offer analysis services such as feasibility, litigation review, or forensics, in addition to normal building design services.
- Firms that have a home office with several branches in other cities or countries.
- Closer partnership with construction manager firms and clients using Building Information Modeling (BIM).

Architectural firms in the future will organize themselves into whatever form best delivers their services.

Chapter Nine: Records

Paper beginning,
Brick and mortar a lifetime.
Paper forever.

Architects were problem solvers who designed custom made buildings. The process required the production of documents and records on paper.

In the 50s and 60s, required documents consisted of drawings and specifications and not much else. The drawing phases were schematics (SC), design development (DD), and construction documents (CD). Specifications were written during the CD phase. Engineers made calculations by hand on letter sized paper. Very few other design documents were prepared.

Multiple copies of the CDs were printed for bidding and construction. The selected contractor received a few more sets. During construction the contractor submitted shop drawings and other written information indicating compliance to the contract documents. That was it.

Project "deliverables", of course, increased in quantity due to increased complexity of buildings, business practices, regulations, legal requirements, agency and client reviews, and the cloud of litigation. All were collected until the project was complete.

When the project was complete, the documents were retained by the architect primarily for pride of authorship and claim of ownership. The ownership claim became a subject of dispute with clients who felt, and often had it written into the contract, that the original drawings belonged to the project owner. Architects were concerned that an unscrupulous client (not theirs, of course) would provide their drawings to another architect for use on another or later project. They feared the future architect (probably a "plan stamper" type), would change only the title block and claim the design was his own. Architects not only did not want their creative design "stolen", they did not want to be liable for work over which they had no control or received no fee. They kept the originals.

In the early years of CAD, ownership and control of electronic drawing files was the concern. When issued as CAD files in .dwg format, information was even more vulnerable to change, whether deliberate or unintended, than were original pencil tracings. Disclaimers and hold harmless statements and waivers usually accompanied their issue. The concern relaxed in later years because either security hadn't turned out to be a significant issue, or offices considered the enforcement effort was not beneficial.

The primary control of liability resided with signed and sealed paper copies. As long as they would be a requirement for any new building permit, liability would be vested in the new signer.

Gradually, retention of and responsibility for all of the project records defaulted to the architect. In the "paper days", the original tracings were considered the most valuable. Offices retained an archive as record documents (sometimes called "as-builts"). The project specifications were also kept as part of the record documents.

An architect's demeanor was not conducive to the effort to clean up, close out, and maintain all the accumulated records at the end of a project. Most preferred to start new projects; few want to finish the last one. Claiming that storage space was cheaper than time, they boxed up the records and went on to the next job.

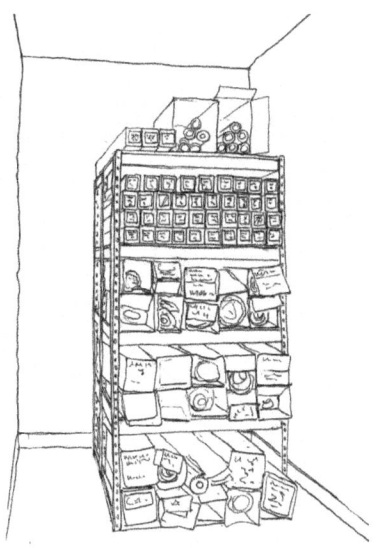

Drawings in Tube Files

Storage was complicated by differences of shape. Drawings were kept either in flat files or were rolled and stored in bins; specifications stored on shelves in a separate location. Specs, considered less valuable as a record than drawings, tended to become neglected.

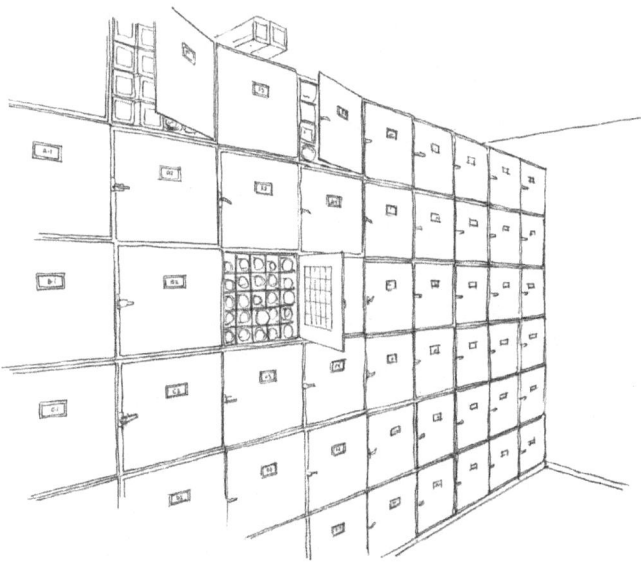

Tracings Stored in Tubes in Vault

Specifications Stored on Shelves in Vault

The remainder of the paperwork was usually discarded. Schematic and design development drawings were thrown out, although designers insisted that some of their renderings be retained as artwork. Shop drawings were sometimes kept for the archives. Since they were folded blue-line prints, a different shape than either tracings or specs, shop drawings presented the same problem of becoming separated. Some offices went to the trouble of microfilming and cataloging the record documents, but more declined when they learned its expense.

Size and shape of the various paper documents for proper retention was not just a silly concern. File storage furniture was designed for size and shape categories: drawing files or letter files. Drawings for a project were stored with drawings for other projects, specs for a project with specs for others, not with each other.

Architectural offices sometimes made mild attempts to unify, including the practice of publishing the specs on the drawings themselves. This practice eliminated one of the different formats, but spec writers and their clerical assistants were accustomed to typewriters and word processors. It did not catch hold as a general practice.

The military drawing sheet size of 22 x 34 inches, allowing as it did printing and storing half-sized drawings on 11 x 17 inch paper, was an attempt to simplify the issue, but file cabinets for that size were not available. The drawings were still stored in flat files; the specs on shelves or in file cabinets.

Another retention decision for architects was whether or not to keep consultant's drawings. Engineers had their own pride of authorship and concerns about control of the originals, so the architect who wanted a complete record retained only a copy.

Documents were retained not only for the record but for reference on later work. Reference value was achieved only in direct proportion to its accessibility. Drawings of recent past projects

Chapter Nine: Records

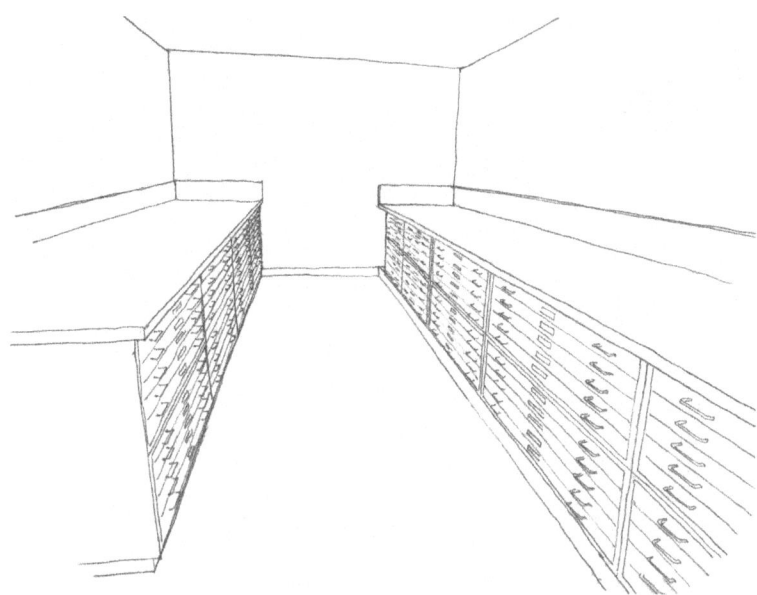

Drawing Storage in Flat Files

were kept in flat files close to the drafting room in the same drawer they occupied during the design phase. Older projects were stored remotely. Periodically (when the boss got frustrated and declared a clean-out day) there would be a rotation shuffle to clean out the nearby drawers to make room for current projects.

The category that saw the most growth was project records other than drawings and specs. The list included literally any and every document sent or received during the progress of a project: correspondence, agreements and contracts, meeting minutes and memos, basis of design documents, owner directives, construction phase transmittals, applications for payment, copies of contracts, code research notes, proposal requests, copies of e-mails, change orders, and close-out documents, to name a few. Most were retained.

One reason for the accumulation was to avoid spending time to sort out important from trivial, a distinction probably not revealed until much later. The primary reason was to insulate against litigation.

Architects, like other professionals, practiced somewhat defensively in the age of litigation. They had enough bad experience with delay claims to appreciate the value of records that proved they performed their tasks in a timely manner (provided they actually did). Business office records grew as much, if not more, as tax laws and employment regulations became more complex.

When the piles of boxes became too big to ignore they became the subject of discussions of how long to keep the records and whether to keep them at all. Laws and rules advising retention periods were numerous and vague, with opinions varying from 3 years to 10 years. Rules also offered various understandings of "statutes of limitation" and their enforcement. By the time any such statute may have expired, the project records were probably neither intact nor labeled well enough to reliably identify for disposal.

Project Files in Stacked Boxes

Then there was always the fear that as soon as they were disposed, even if beyond any realistic statute expiration, the trial lawyer would call and the architect's defense would not be there. On the other hand, neither would any incriminating evidence.

Also, a client might call with prospects for a remodeling or addition to the former project, and it would be awfully good to have a copy of the original floor plans or the structural shop drawings. So with uncertainty the piles grew.

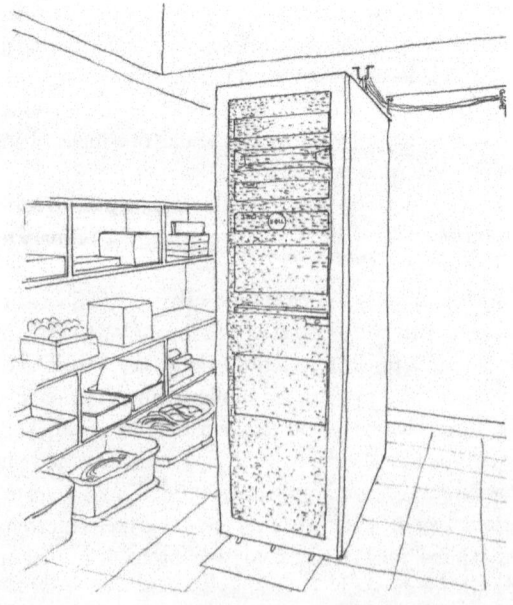

Local Area Network Server

Chapter Nine: Records

The shift to electronic documents lessened the accumulation of paper to some extent.

However, many architects managed their projects using duplicate paper copies. Oriented to the spatial, tactile environment, they found it more effective to organize and retrieve references from a file drawer or bookshelf than a virtual image from a computer. It required self-discipline to part with the paper library when the project closed out, otherwise the pile continued to grow.

Complete conversion to electronic media was accomplished, but insecurity about electronic records lurked behind a completely paperless practice. The cemetery of outdated media devices haunted a confident commitment. Many offices probably still had floppy discs stored somewhere that they planned to convert some day. Since computers were no longer available with floppy disc drives (where did all the A and B drives go?), they will in the future not have D and E drives for compact discs either. Many of the current file formats, PDF, JPEG, TIF, .dwg file, etc, may not be around in the future.

An office could maintain a museum of old reading devices to access the old record formats, but probably didn't. For records retention, low tech was best. For sound it was 78 rpm sound records; they could be played manually using a needle and a paper cone. For drawings it was paper. Massive off-site electronic storage, open source, and the "cloud" offered a vision for long term storage in the future. Meanwhile, the default was a paper copy.

Retention of renderings and models was another consideration. Archive quality renderings were framed and displayed in the owner's or the architect's office. In either location, however, sooner or later the issue of permanent retention would arise. The architect may move to a new location, acquire successor partners, or close altogether. The choices were: 1) keep and continue to maintain the work, 2) donate it to an institutional archive, or 3) photograph the work and dispose of the original. Choice 3 was the usual selection, with or without the photos.

Study models were usually disposed shortly after the project was complete. Exceptions were made for the work of prominent architects like Frank Gehry and Louis Kahn, whose design process models could and did become the feature of museum exhibitions.

Expensive realistic models with plexiglass covers made for significant projects required an investment of space and upkeep. Considered too valuable to simply dispose, they sometimes remained on a coffee table in the architect's front office until moved to a back office where they stayed until major clean-out day. If the owner kept the model it would receive the same consideration. The dumpster decision was best made administratively; the architect who had "ownership" of the design and construction of the model did not have the heart to order its disposal. It was like personally ordering the demolition of his or her favorite building.

When and if a building itself was demolished the issue of what to do with its records remained. If it had sentimental or historic value its records did also. Provisions would be made in the demolition order to either take new archive-quality photos of the building (if its condition allowed), or to provide for preservation and maintenance of previous photos.

The best record of a building was the architectural drawings, especially the floor plans, elevations, and sections. If hand-drawn, the original tracings were preserved. Whether drawn by hand or computer, the drawings were kept as an archive.

A lasting solution to the retention of architectural records, whether or not the building was significant, was to have the work published in a bound book. Having the record of one's work maintained in libraries (by others) for future generations was the dream of many. The architect's storeroom could then safely be cleared.

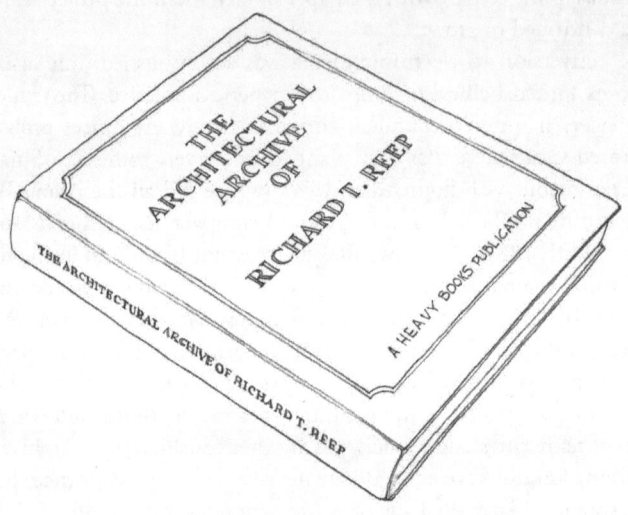

Archive in Bound Book Format

Chapter Ten: Design

The hungry child cries.
Milk is in the mother's breast.
They come together

Design, the process, has three "dimensions": a need, a resource, and an action. A person is hungry, bread and peanut butter are on the table, a sandwich is made and eaten. A prairie family needs shelter, sod and metal tools are at hand, a man cuts the sod and lays it into walls. Change in any one of the dimensions changes the outcome. If the person has a spiritual hunger instead of bodily hunger, the sandwich may be an icon. If, instead of peanut butter there is meat, the meal has a different flavor and nutritional result. If the builder becomes exhausted, the prairie house may have a lower roof line.

This definition of design is not unique to architecture. It is inherent in any creative process. In fact, every problem-solving activity can be viewed as a creative process. Architects may not be conscious of the elements while designing, but an awareness of their existence is helpful. When stuck on an issue, one could ask: Have I understood the client's needs correctly? Are these materials really going to hold up? Would a study model reveal the spatial relationships better than a drawing? Awareness of the three dimensions is a process approach to design.

Design, the academic discipline, leaped over this elemental analysis. Architectural schools took their students directly to form as a basis for design, while on the way acknowledging that "form follows function". Function was narrowly defined as practical and mechanical aspects, but could also include spiritual goals as well as basic shelter requirements, social as well as personal objectives. These would all be stated in the project program as needs. Construction materials and methods were the resources. The construction industry provided the action.

The application of appropriate form was a daunting challenge for beginning students with little or no foundation in architecture. Their design approach was influenced by, in addition to the program, the design trends of the day. Several design trends named as academic theories or styles have been prominent. Modern was the first in this era.

Students entering the field in the 1950s were provided a clear understanding of the place and purpose of architectural design: Modern Architecture. Modern, also called Contemporary or International, was a theory, a style, the definition of an era, a process, and in some ways a liturgy. It was unquestionably "the way" to becoming an architect. Modern became the base line from which later architectural theories evolved. Its era has passed, but it continues to be a strong influence.

The faculty in most schools of architecture was influenced by the legacy of both the Ecole des Beaux-Arts and Modern. The older members had probably been educated in the Beaux-Arts tradition prevalent in American schools of architecture in the first half of the 20th century. The younger, many of whom had served in World War II, arrived in the late 40s after having been educated in Ivy League or Chicago schools. They followed the teaching methods of the Bauhaus, especially its basic design values of unity, variety, and balance. Like their predecessors at the Bauhaus, they embraced the polemic of Modern Architecture.

Received by the students as a liturgy, the catechism of Modern produced building masses separated into pure rectangular boxes. A small box adjoining a larger box was separated by a connecting element so they each retained their 6-sided identity. Detailing of intersections and connections was subjected to the same esthetic scrutiny as major parts. The boxes were formed of sticks and planes—sticks for the framing members and window frames, and planes for the level roof, walls, and windows, although the roof may be sloped to form a shed shape. Wall elements were rectangles. Trim was disdained. Flush doors replaced stile and rail doors. Windows were floor-to-ceiling or not at all. Punched openings were not in the vocabulary. Brick was acceptable for its "human scale" qualities and because Mies used it, even though it recalled the hand craftsmanship of the old days.

This rather superficial view of Modern had a deeper basis founded in the philosophical premise that art imitates life, a premise that has since been challenged but at that time was idealistically accepted. Art in this regard is reason. Life is nature. In spite of all of the horrible things the world had recently witnessed, people carried a fundamental belief that there was an underlying natural goodness in mankind. It had gone awry due to evil forces of reason, but goodness could still be found, given an optimistic outlook and a diligent search.

Architects who believed that the forms of the past represented the society that had gone awry developed what became called Modern Architecture. They searched for the fundamental, natural origins of architectural form. Rather than referring to the forms of previous societies, they believed the form of an object must follow its intended function. A building must express the needs, not the status, of the user. Its materials, structure and shape must express its purpose or program. A wall was designed only to keep out the weather, provide privacy and security, support the roof, or some other function, expressing those basic purposes and those only.

The same analytical rigor was applied to other components. Structural elements were sized only as required to perform the function and were exposed. Any element other than what was inherent in the fundamental purpose was "applied decoration". "Artificial" and "preconception" were common pejorative terms. Students used Louis Sullivan's quote, "Form forever follows function" as a sound bite.

Le Corbusier's "worker housing" projects in Pessac and Paris were prime references. His later Villa Savoye in France and Walter Gropius' Bauhaus school in Dessau in the 1920s became icons of the period.

The post-war period provided the energy to break with the past now that the Great Depression and the World War II were over. Modern architecture expressed this energy, just as its predecessor, the Bauhaus, had expressed the societal changes from Imperialism toward democratization in early 20th century Europe.

On graduation from architecture school these new crusaders found that clients, especially residential, were not "ready" for Modern no matter how many sermons about its correctness. Its severity was not an easy sell to a couple that just wanted a comfortable home (except when the architect was his own client and he had to convince only his wife). Floor-to-ceiling windows and flat roofs were not attractive to homeowners who lived through long harsh northern winters. Students and young architects in the north envied those in Florida when reading about Paul Rudolph and the Sarasota School in Progressive Architecture, and in Los Angeles in Arts + Architecture magazine's Case Study Houses.

Chapter Ten: Design

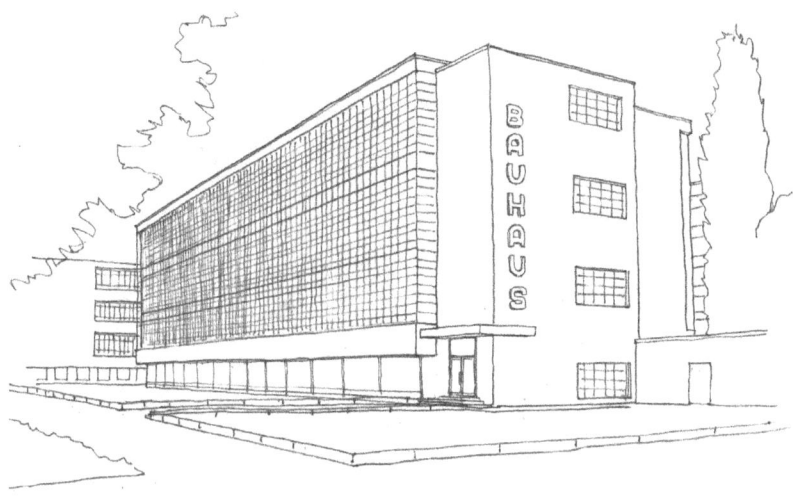

**Bauhaus, Dessau, Germany, 1926.
Walter Gropius, architect**

**Villa Savoye, Poissy, 1931.
Le Corbusier, architect**

They admired Mies van der Rohe's Farnsworth House in Plano, Illinois for its spare forms, even though Mies's use of refined materials to conceal structural elements contradicted their understanding of the industrial design goals Gropius had brought to the Bauhaus. Mies applied a classy approach to Modern, dressing his forms in formal attire. Bauhaus in a tuxedo.

Accompanying this trend to Modern, and in many cases directing it, were several societal factors: increased prosperity and industrialization, increased number and variety of new building projects, and overall optimism in the future of America. Prosperity and

**Farnsworth Residence, Plano, Illinois, 1951.
Ludwig Mies van der Rohe, architect**

industrialization led to more shopping centers, offices, and factories, which Modern Architecture suited well. Buildings were designed rapidly and used materials common with the industrial economy—steel, concrete, concrete block, plywood, glass, and aluminum. Increases in families meant increases in the number of children and therefore schools, another building type well suited to Modern.

Modern Architecture was acceptable for most non-residential projects but in its pure form it was subject to criticism and even ridicule. The general public just "didn't like it". It was too stark, too flat, cold, empty, inhuman. It's severe forms didn't look like "nature". Clients were not ready to discard the symbols of past times. Modern was not working for anyone but architects.

While the purists insisted on more austerity (less is more), others began to soften the images. Designs by Edward D. Stone and Minoru Yamasaki in the early 1960s added textural forms and screens to their façades. The designs became the subject of much debate between Modernists, who dismissed them as applied decoration, and the public, which accepted them as pleasing.

Frank Lloyd Wright, though in his later years, was still a strong influence on young architects, especially in the Midwest where many living examples of his work were within reach. Wright's work was acceptably Modern; integrating sloping roofs and natural materials like native stone and wood into free-flowing floor plans and thematic spatial compositions. His insistence that architecture be "organic" was accessible to Modernists searching for the source of form.

The hero of Modern Architecture, at least to other architects in the 1960s, was Louis Kahn. His work reinforced belief in the fundamental nature of materials, structure, light and space, and of the aspirations of mankind. He proved that the architect, emotionally and intellectually prepared, could draw from that inner nature and express it beautifully through architecture. Recall Kahn's teachings, many of which were presented in Jan C. Rowan's article "Wanting to Be - The Philadelphia School" (Progressive Architecture, April, 1961):

Chapter Ten: Design

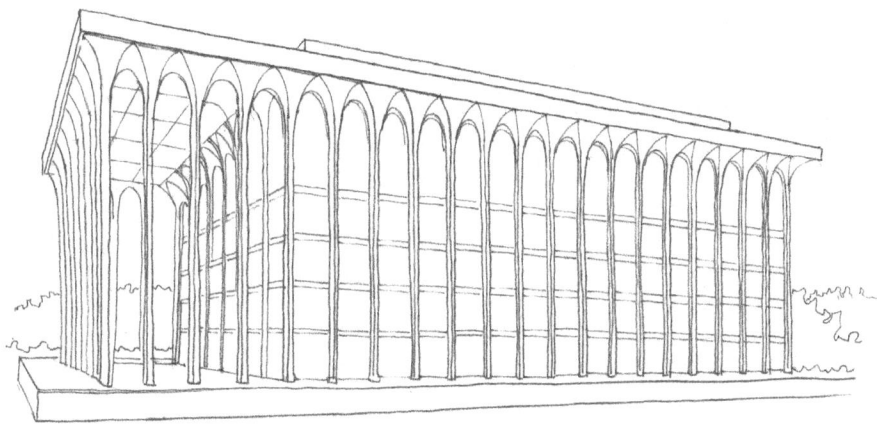

**Northwestern Life Insurance Building, Minneapolis, 1964.
Minoru Yamasaki**

**Falling Water, Mill Run, Pennsylvania, 1937.
Frank Lloyd Wright**

- Wanting to be ("I asked the brick what it wanted to be").
- Search to understand and express the nature of light, structure, site, and the broad purpose and meaning of the building.
- Form is the determinant of Design. Form is the desire, the nature of the need. Design is the expression, the physical manifestation of Form. Form comes first, Design follows. Hunger is Form, the spoon is Design. (Note the new definition of Form in contrast to Sullivan's.)

- Use of structural elements to express design.
- Served and servant spaces identified (a Beaux Arts tenet) and expressed as architecture (a Modern concept).
- Search for the "seed" (or DNA in today's terms) from which the design concept begins.

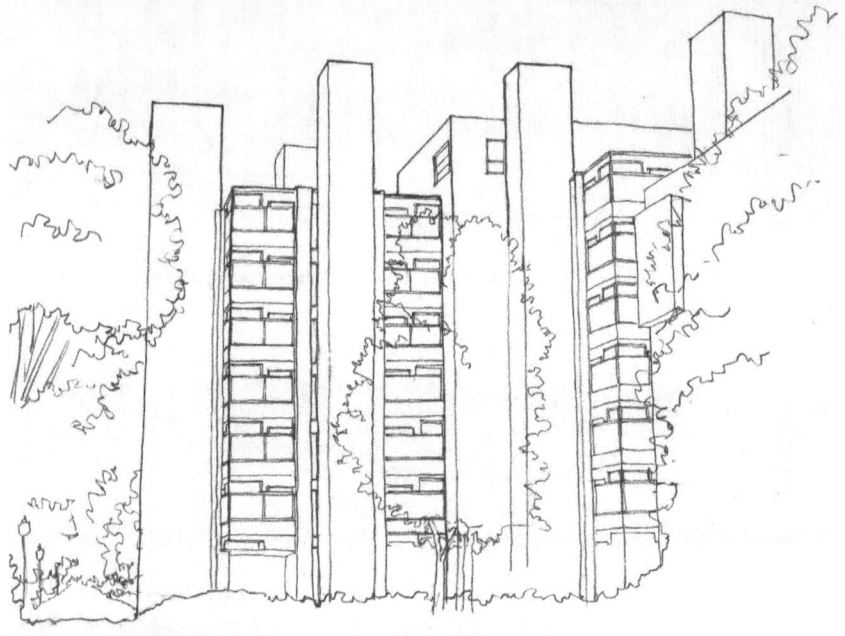

**Richards Medical Research Laboratories, Philadelphia, 1960.
Louis I. Kahn, architect**

Lou Kahn was the most romantic, most poetic, Modern Architect. He was also the last. His era witnessed the paradigm shift from the innocent belief that art imitates life to the more worldly belief that life imitates art. Oscar Wilde had predicted it in 1889. Because of affluence, behavioral science, media, and consumerism, society came to believe and behave as if there was nothing really natural in the world. Nature was considered to be only what each of us perceived it to be. Experience determined perception and perception influenced experience. The noble savage was an invention of arrogant "enlightened" man. Psychiatrists insisted there were no accidents. Situation ethics prevailed. The medium was the message.

Even Kahn admitted that sometimes the sight of a spoon can make a person hungry. His brick replied, "What do you want me to be?"

Architects got busy. They required a constant supply of new images and forms to keep up with the commissions for all the new building types in an affluent society. Some tried to copy Kahn's medium, even if they missed his message, but found his designs too limiting and his thoughtful process too slow for everyday commercial projects. Worse, clients wouldn't accept the Modern catechism any longer. They even demanded their roofs have gables and hips and overhangs.

Corporations discovered their image could be enhanced with a high-tech façade designed by a well-known architect. Air conditioning components had to be concealed behind suspended ceilings. Fluorescent lights were economical and efficient, though not romantic. Office workers enjoyed colors other than black, gray, and white. Carpeting became the preferred floor covering. Interior Design was born as a new discipline. Landscape Architects used the products of nature to soften building edges.

Robert Venturi, a young colleague of Kahn's, showed how to loosen up the image, how to make a sloped roof look Modern, a thin wall have interest, a double hung window acceptable. His palette permitted gable roofs, punched windows, manipulation of the façade, and even applied decoration, all while maintaining references to Modern. For those who didn't want their peers to think they were selling out, Venturi offered academic credentials and the polemics that "less is a bore" and "art is everywhere—learn from it", salted not with cynicism but with irony. The irony helped ease the transition out of innocence. Venturi's forms were labeled Post Modern.

Early Post Modern building designs were characterized by elementary child-like massing: no overhangs, pastel colors, applied decoration, primary-shaped windows such as circles. Two-dimensional cutouts of classical motifs were applied like stage decoration to an otherwise Modern façade.

Architects took delight in the Post Modern design process. Owners, relieved of the austerity of Modern, enjoyed the new images. Michael Graves' Portland Municipal Services Building offered an example. The design received an honor award in 1983 from the American Institute of Architects.

**Vanna Venturi House, Philadelphia, 1964.
Robert Venturi, architect**

Post Modern is a term applied to any number of current activities which besides architecture include most of the other arts. It is loosely defined as anything that is not Modern, is not quite radical, and needs a group identity. The term continues to be included in the architectural style folio in that manner.

**Portland Municipal Services Building, 1982.
Michael Graves, architect**

In another branch of design following Modern, Kahn's and Corbu's exposed concrete designs evolved into what was called Brutalist. Kallman, McKinnell & Knowles' competition-winning design in 1962 for the Boston City Hall is an example. Moshe Safdie, another Kahn successor, expanded the potential of concrete in the Habitat project in Montreal in 1967. Entire rooms and apartments were built of concrete on the ground, then set one on another to form a building.

These works offered monumental images and gravitas to institutional and residential projects. Exposed concrete, however, had several practical limits: it did not keep out the elements unless it had a sturdy coating that contradicted its raw image; thermal insulation had to be added to the inner surface, making the wall even thicker; and it required expensive formwork which was almost like constructing two buildings and discarding one. Also, people rejected the heavy, brutal appearance.

A number of architects in the mid 1960s saw the need for a more rational approach to design. Noting there seemed to be an excess of "form-making" without meaning, they searched the fields of behavioral science, industrial design and mathematics for determinants of form.

At the Association of Collegiate Schools of Architecture (ASCA) teacher's conference at Cranbrook in 1966, behavioral scientist Larry Summers presented research into human responses to color, space, and each other. Bruce Archer described how the field of industrial design applied systems analysis and ergonomics to the design process. Christopher Alexander explored how mathematical analysis could determine architectural form, as published in his Notes on the Synthesis of Form (Harvard University Press, 1964), and later developed at Berkeley the tools of Pattern Language.

**Habitat, Montreal, 1967.
Moshe Safdie, architect.**

Edward T. Hall in his book The Hidden Dimension (Doubleday, 1966) increased awareness of spatial relationships between people.

None of these studies led directly to architecture, but all were very influential in developing its rational side. Rationality was also influencing other fields such as education, environmental science, and computer science.

The rational approach required that previous assumptions and precepts be analyzed and deconstructed. When applied to architectural form the process provided almost total design freedom. Physical laws of gravity and weather, and to some extent human behavior, provided the only limits.

The approach was given a name in the exhibition at the Museum of Modern Art in 1988. Calling it Deconstructivist Architecture, Decon for short, curators Philip Johnson and Mark Wigley featured the current work of Coop Himmelblau, Peter Eisenman, Frank Gehry, Zaha M. Hadid, Rem Koolhaas, Daniel Libeskind, and Bernard Tschumi.

The press release of the MOMA exhibition summarized the common attributes of the work in the exhibition:

Deconstructivist Architecture focuses on seven international architects whose recent work marks the emergence of a new sensibility in architecture. The architects recognize the imperfectability of the modern world and seek to address, in

Johnson's words, the "pleasures of unease." Obsessed with diagonals, arcs, and warped planes, they intentionally violate the cubes and right angles of modernism. Their projects continue the experimentation with structure initiated by the Russian Constructivists, but the goal of perfection of the 1920s is subverted. The traditional virtues of harmony, unity, and clarity are displaced by disharmony, fracturing, and mystery.

The statement illustrated another attribute of Deconstructivism: obscurity. If a project was founded in rational de-construction, the resulting re-construction didn't present an ordered solution. One questioned why the nihilistic outlook. Disharmony and fracturing were artistic themes better suited to the media of music, art and literature rather than the capital-intense public realm of architecture.

Another attribute of Decon was excess. Its influence and acceptance was accompanied by and dependent on prosperity in the western world which allowed for the exorbitant budgets the projects required.

Later examples of Decon may not have been progeny of the rational approach. Peter Eisenman, for example, related his source to the linguistic studies of Jacques Derrida rather than the design rationalists[1]. Frank Gehry's work seemed to be inspired by form-making, not theory [2].

The MOMA exhibit was an example of how architectural theories originate and evolve. Modern had emerged from the Bauhaus as a straightforward practical solution to industrial society's needs. It was identified as a theory by academics like Sigfried Giedion, Vincent Scully, Christopher Jencks, Kenneth Frampton and others.

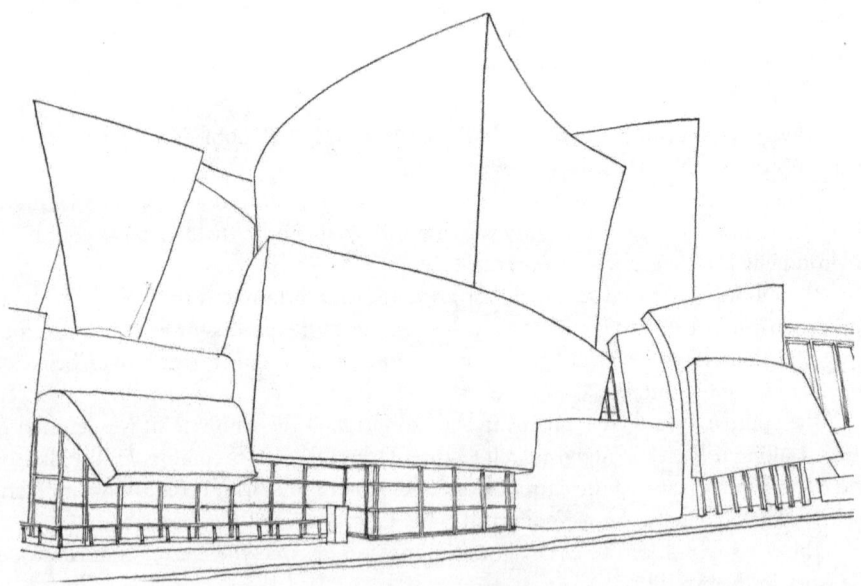

Walt Disney Concert Hall, Los Angeles, 2003.
Frank Gehry, architect.

The architectural press championed Modern until well into the 70s. The previously mentioned Progressive Architecture and Art+Architecture magazines were two of the leaders, joined monthly by Architectural Record, The AIA Journal, Architectural Forum, Architectural Review, Domus, and several others.

Academia did not embrace Post Modern as a theory, except for the work and writing of Robert Venturi. It did go all out for Decon in the 80s and early 90s, providing academic legitimacy for the urge to break away from Modern[3]. Currently, academia is focused more on social issues than design theories.

The architectural press, like all print media, has dwindled in both quantity and influence. Of the previous list only Architectural Record remains. The currently remaining publications that represent general practice, Architectural Record and Architect, cover significant projects of the leading architects, but like academia focus primarily on social issues of energy conservation and sustainability.

Sustainability as a focus of design traces its origins to the late 50s when Ian McHarg, Chair of the Department of Landscape Architecture at the University of Pennsylvania, pioneered ecological planning. His work and teaching, stated clearly in his landmark book "Design with Nature" (Doubleday and Company, 1969) and the subsequent work of his students were forerunners of today's environmental movement.

The currently recognized "starchitects", most of whom emerged in the Decon days, have set aside whatever "fracturing" they may have produced. Their work could be called functional sculpture – functional in that it has a stated program and sculptural in that it has irrational forms. In that regard they have joined in Frank Gehry's search for form. The primary building types for their work are museums, libraries, performing arts facilities, and high rise buildings. No name has been given for this theory yet, so perhaps it can be called Post Decon.

At this writing the construction industry in all building types has been quiet for several years. It may be a long time before the prosperity of the last decades of the 20th and first of the the 21st century returns. One may speculate whether Decon and its successor styles will return with their previous creative energy. It may depend on when and whether economic and social order recover.

The current emphasis for practitioners, at least for government work, is for buildings to be leaders in the conservation of energy. These are the types of commercial projects receiving recognition.

Design trends can be related to the tools used to produce them. Architectural design, up until 3D CAD came along, was produced primarily with 2 dimensional graphics – orthographic views. It is not surprising that these tools produced buildings that had orderly floor plans, studied elevations and organized massing.

But humans do not experience buildings orthographically. Graphic tools that allow easy study of the third dimension will inevitably allow architects to find ways to explore space and form in new ways. Decon, with its exuberant forms, paralleled the transition from hand drawing to CAD and early forays into 3D CAD. Widespread use of 3D CAD will influence architectural design in the future.

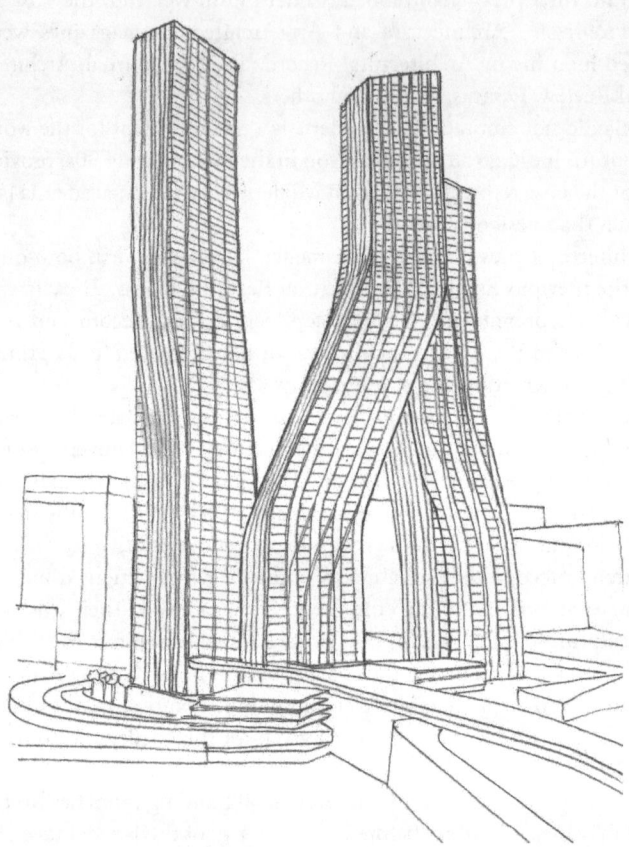

**Signature Towers, Dubai, proposed.
Zaha Hadid, architect**

Through all of these periods and evolutions of theory and style, the catechism of Modern Architecture maintained its grip on design until well into the 1970s. Some devout firms would seriously consider declining a potential commercial commission whose owner dictated it be designed in a certain not-Modern style like French Provincial. Attitudes softened in the 80s when style, an attribute prominent in the auto and fashion industries, became openly discussed and accepted in architecture. Architects joined the commercial world.

The styles currently seen include: Modern and Post Modern (for commercial and institutional), Post Decon (for museums, libraries, performing arts, and high rises), Minimalism (for residences), Cracker and California (for residences), Southwestern (for shopping malls), and Continental (for high-end hospitality), to name only a few. But in reality anything goes. Architectural design awards tend to favor Minimalist design, the descendent of Modern, suggesting that Modern is still considered by award-givers as the only true architecture.

Modern continues its influence on architects even now. A common element of most successful buildings is still the value placed on the basic design tenets of Modern Architecture: clear floor plans, clarity of massing, orderly facades, quality materials, and good detailing. Unity, variety, and balance.

Notes

1. "The main channel from deconstructivist philosophy to architectural theory was through the philosopher Jacques Derrida's influence with Peter Eisenman." Source: http://en.wikipedia.org/w/index.php?oldid=422357231
2. "I'll take materials around me, materials on my table, and work with them as I'm searching for an idea that works." Frank Gehry Talks Frankly. Playboy Magazine Interviews Architect Frank Gehry. January 2011
3. The attempt in deconstructivism throughout is to move architecture away from what its practitioners see as the constricting 'rules' of modernism such as "form follows function," "purity of form," and "truth to materials." Source: http://en.wikipedia.org/w/index.php?oldid=422357231

A Note on the Author

Richard Reep's career in architecture began more than 60 years ago with a Bachelor of Architecture degree from the University of Minnesota. Following graduation from the University of Pennsylvania in Louis Kahn's Master's Studio, Richard joined the faculty at Clemson University School of Architecture, rising to Associate Professor. He helped shape the syllabus for the School's change from a 5- to a 6-year curriculum.

In addition to teaching, Richard has practiced with firms in Minneapolis, St. Paul, Chicago, St. Louis, and, for the past 40 years, with KBJ Architects, Inc. in Jacksonville, Florida where he serves as Principal Emeritus. His experience includes designer and team leader for college facilities, high rise office buildings, airport terminals, resort hotels, medical facilities, religious institutions, and many others.

Richard Sr. has been active with the American Institute of Architects, the AIA, serving as president of the Jacksonville chapter and president of AIA Florida.

He likes to write songs and light verse. He and his wife Reagan enjoy ballroom dancing and playing with their grandchildren. Their two sons, Richard and John, are both practicing architects.

www.ingramcontent.com/pod-product-compliance
Lightning Source LLC
Chambersburg PA
CBHW031125160426
43192CB00008B/1110